Compiler Tom Nuttall was the senior and online editor of *Prospect* magazine and compiled the 'In fact' column for seven years.

Prospect is Britain's premier monthly journal of politics and culture. Launched in 1995 by its present editor, former *Financial Times* correspondent David Goodhart, *Prospect* has acquired a reputation as the most intelligent magazine of current affairs and cultural debate in Britain.

in fact

You are One-Third Daffodil
and other facts to turn your
world upside down

From the pages of Prospect magazine
Compiled by Tom Nuttall

preface
publishing

This paperback edition published by Preface 2009

10 9 8 7 6 5 4 3

Copyright © Prospect Publishing Ltd 2008, 2009

Prospect Publishing Ltd has asserted the right to be identified as the author of this work
under the Copyright, Designs and Patents Act 1988

First published in Great Britain in 2008 by Preface Publishing
1 Queen Anne's Gate
London SWIH 9BT

An imprint of The Random House Group Limited

www.rbooks.co.uk
www.prefacepublishing.co.uk

Addresses for companies within The Random House Group Limited
can be found at www.randomhouse.co.uk

The Random House Group Limited Reg. No. 954009

A CIP catalogue record for this book is available from the British Library

ISBN 978 1 84809 003 3

Penguin Random House is committed to a sustainable future for
our business, our readers and our planet. This book is made from
Forest Stewardship Council® certified paper.

Designed and typeset in Adobe Garamond by
Strathmore Publishing Services, London ECI
www.strathmorepublishing.co.uk

Printed and bound in Great Britain by Clays Ltd, St Ives plc

contents

Acknowledgements   vii
Introduction   ix

1.   SOCIAL STANDING   1

2.   IN PERSPECTIVE   39

3.   BE VERY AFRAID   57

4.   HOW THE WORLD WORKS   71

5.   GONE TO THE DOGS   79

6.   FUNNY FOREIGNERS   91

7.   THE PAST IS ANOTHER COUNTRY   105

8.   DOUBLE TAKE   115

9.   FUNNY OLD WORDS   131

10.   REASONS TO BE CHEERFUL   139

11.   TRUE STORIES   149

12.   CURIOUSER AND CURIOUSER   171

acknowledgements

Thanks first to my colleagues at *Prospect* – this book is theirs as much as it is mine. David Goodhart invented the 'In fact' column and continues to act as fact filterer-in-chief. Susha Lee-Shothaman's fact radar is even more finely tuned than my own. And I salute the anonymous army of editorial assistants and interns whose labours kept 'In fact' going for six years before I arrived at *Prospect*, and on whose factual shoulders I stand.

Without John Kelly, this book would not have appeared. Trevor Dolby at Preface got the project off the ground and has been helpful and encouraging throughout. Talitha Hitchcock and the team at Strathmore Publishing made the book beautiful and handled my endless rounds of tedious edits with splendid forbearance.

Finally, it's a great pleasure to say that any factual errors in this book are not the responsibility of the author.

introduction

'Facts are stupid things,' President Ronald Reagan told the Republican National Convention in 1988. And in the six years I have been compiling the 'In fact' column for *Prospect*, I've sometimes felt the same. Yet for the most part we tend to revere facts; they drive scientific development, they fuel political debate, they fill up amusing books like this one. (Even Reagan was actually a fact fan. He had meant to tell his fellow Republicans that facts were 'stubborn' things; it just came out wrong.)

A fact can, of course, be a slippery thing. Shorn of context, it can lend undeserved authority to a shoddy opinion; artfully combined with other carefully selected particulars, it can crowd out dissent. And despite our claims to the contrary, it's not always so clear that we do respect the things. Nine times out of ten, if someone writes in to *Prospect* accusing an article of getting its facts wrong, they actually turn out to be flustered not about the facts themselves, but what the author has chosen to do with them.

The 'In fact' column traces its ancestry back to the very first issues of *Prospect*. It was inspired by the famous 'Index' from the American monthly magazine *Harper's*, which typically combines a string of thematically connected facts, usually numerical, to cajole the reader into seeing the world the *Harper's* way. *Prospect's* 'In fact', on the other hand, holds the facts themselves in esteem: their neutrality, their seriousness, sometimes their downright weirdness.

'In fact' is, admittedly, insulated from criticism by its cunning device of always attributing facts to third-party sources (the eagle-eyed reader may on occasion pause over the meaning of 'Prospect research'). We take a 'third-way' approach to the question of whether the facts themselves are 'true', triangulating between old-fashioned objectivism and postmodern relativism. 'In fact' is, ironically, the only section of *Prospect* which isn't fact-checked, but at the same time we aim only to feature facts which have at least the whiff of truth about them. More importantly, rather like *Prospect* itself, the column cleaves to no particular ideology and seeks only to publish the original, the provocative and the stimulating (and, now and then, the crude).

If 'In fact' has ever aimed to do anything beyond amuse and astound, it is perhaps to get you to see the world slightly differently. For instance, does it not present the Israeli–Palestinian conflict in a different light when you realise that the areas under dispute – the West Bank and the Gaza strip – are roughly the same size as, respectively, Lincolnshire and Sheffield? Or what about the strange shock to one's historical sense that comes from learning that Galileo was offered an academic seat at Harvard (he turned it down)?

Prospect readers often tell me that 'In fact' is the part of the magazine they turn to first each month. In my early days at *Prospect*, as an editorial assistant with little influence over the rest of the magazine, I got a real kick out of comments like this. I was even known to exclaim that 'In fact' represented the 'essence' of *Prospect*; after all, didn't articles sometimes get edited down to short diary items, and didn't diary items sometimes get compressed into single facts?

Still, this hubris didn't prepare me for what happened one day in January 2003. We were wrapping up the latest issue of *Prospect*; it was 1 a.m., the magazine had to go to the printers that night and, as usual, I was floundering around for facts to fill the column. Desperate to allow my superiors to get to bed, I turned to the fact source of last resort: Google. A search for, I think, 'interesting facts' led me to an American student's personal website. And there, nestling like a pearl among photos of boozy nights out and lists of favourite bands, I saw it: 'Most toilets flush in E flat.' Perfect. Alas, *Prospect*'s high standards for sources meant I wouldn't be able to credit my saviour (and I hadn't invented 'Prospect research' yet), and so I was forced to seek out a mainstream alternative; Google helpfully led me to the slightly sinister-sounding US 'Centres for Disease Control and Prevention.' Job done.

The issue was published a few days later. I was taking a well-deserved day off and enjoying a lie-in when I was woken by the squeal of my mobile phone. I answered blearily and found myself in conversation with an excitable producer from *Johnny Vaughan Tonight* who wanted to know everything about the toilet fact: where did I get it from? Was it really true? Had I verified it? I patiently directed her to the disease control website and went back to sleep, pleased to have discovered that the long arms of 'In fact' stretched as far as prime-time television chat shows.

Later that day, idly flicking through the *Guardian*, I was brought up short by the paper's third leading article. Entitled 'Closet composers', it was an elegant meditation on the question of whether the fact that toilets flush in E flat, as revealed in *Prospect*, could shed new light on the provenance of some of history's musical masterpieces. (The paper noted Wagner's claim that the opening passage of the *Ring* cycle, a sustained E flat in the double basses, was inspired by a dream in which he had heard the sound of 'swiftly running water'.)

Already buoyed by the day's brace of triumphs, I made it a hat-trick in the evening when Mark Lawson's *Front Row* decided to send a musicologist armed with a tuning fork into the toilets of Broadcasting House to test the veracity of the claim. (I wasn't exactly surprised when it turned out to be hokum.) So there you go: the power of one fact – or 'fact' – to set the day's news agenda. And from there the fact snowballed into the collective consciousness; even now I occasionally come across it in surprising places. A couple of years ago Classic FM made use of it in an advertising campaign, and apparently it even made it on to the *David Letterman Show* in the US.

These days my fact antennae are finely honed; the era of late-night fact scrambles is long past. In fact, I'm so tuned in to the facts around me that while I was editing the fact selection for this book, I sometimes found myself thinking, 'How interesting, must remember that for the column.' Such assiduousness can bear fruit: I might be having a chat in the pub, for instance, and someone will say, 'Did you know…' – instantly I'm on fact alert. If the claim is interesting and can be corroborated, it's in. And after years of this sort of thing, some of my friends have decided they want a piece of the fun and so they act as my fact scouts – plenty of the facts in this book owe their appearance to such diligence.

To preserve the serendipity of the 'In fact' column, where a fact about farts might snuggle up next to one about trade deficits, the facts in this book are for the most part organised not by subject matter but by, for want of a better term 'effect'. So the first chapter contains facts that are likely to go down well at a dinner party; the second facts that aim to change your perspective on things you thought you knew about, and so on.

Hope you enjoy them. And if your appetite for facts is not sated by this book, you'll find plenty more at **www.infact.org.uk**.

Tom Nuttall

Social STANDING

Facts to help you make friends and
influence people

About one in 150 people have lost a digit.

WIRED NEWS, 2ND JULY 2007

Pink Floyd's Dark Side of the Moon was on the US Billboard top 200 for 740 consecutive weeks.

MOJO, MARCH 1998

18 members of Thatcher cabinets published their memoirs.

SUNDAY TIMES, 28TH OCTOBER 2007

In 2007 a possum broke the world hibernation record, emerging after 367 days.

NEW SCIENTIST, 14TH OCTOBER 2007

About 11 per cent of the British population is left-handed – up from 3 per cent a century ago.

SUNDAY TIMES, 16TH SEPTEMBER 2007

Britons lose 885,000 mobile phone handsets each year by accidentally flushing them down the toilet. 810,000 are left in the pub, 315,000 in taxis and 225,000 on the bus. Pet dogs chew through 58,500 handsets, and another 116,000 go through a cycle in the washing machine.

DAILY MAIL, 4TH JUNE 2007

Enoch Powell studied Urdu in order to further his ambition of becoming viceroy of India.

'LIKE THE ROMAN: THE LIFE OF ENOCH POWELL' BY SIMON HEFFER

Four of the five richest countries in the world by per capita income have populations of less than 5m.

FINANCIAL TIMES, 3RD DECEMBER 2007

Britons eat five times as much chicken as they did 20 years ago.

'PLANET CHICKEN' BY HATTIE ELLIS

In Britain, eight walkers have died as a result of cow stampedes in the past decade.

DAILY MAIL, 29TH OCTOBER 2007

Humans share 35 per cent of their genes with daffodils.

STEVEN ROSE, VALEDICTORY ADDRESS AT OPEN UNIVERSITY

If a CEO suffers the loss of a child, the profitability of his / her company slides by an average 20 per cent over the next two years. The loss of a spouse leads to a fall of about 15 per cent, but the death of a mother-in-law to a rise of 7 per cent.

WALL STREET JOURNAL, 5TH SEPTEMBER 2007

In 2006, 177 British men had cosmetic surgery to reduce their breast size.

HARPER'S, MAY 2007

31 per cent of British men and 19 per cent of women download music at work, while 9 per cent of men and 4 per cent of women download pornography.

DAILY TELEGRAPH, 5TH JUNE 2007

In Britain, 5 per cent of fathers expect to return to having regular sex with their partners within a week of them giving birth – 28 per cent within a month.

BRITISH PUBLIC OPINION

If there was a way to squeeze the empty space out of the atoms in our bodies, the entire human race would fit in the space occupied by one sugar cube.

'QUANTUM THEORY CANNOT HURT YOU' BY MARCUS CHOWN

One in four British people suffers from chronic halitosis.

BRITISH DENTAL ASSOCIATION

In Britain, roads account for 1.5 per cent of all land area.
'TRANSPORT: NECESSITY OR LUXURY?' BY AUSTIN WILLIAMS

Iraq is the most ethnically diverse country in the Arab world.
FOREIGN AFFAIRS, MAY/JUNE 2006

There were 135 reports of UFO sightings in Britain in 2007,
up from 97 in 2006.
THE INDEPENDENT, 8TH FEBRUARY 2008

Tommy Franks, the general who led the US invasion of Iraq in
2003, and Laura Bush attended the same Texas high
school at the same time – but didn't know each other.
NEW YORK TIMES, 23RD MARCH 2003

Moulay Ismail the Bloodthirsty, the last Sharifian emperor
of Morocco, left more offspring – 1,042 at the time of
his death in 1727 – than anyone else on record.
'WHY BEAUTIFUL PEOPLE HAVE MORE DAUGHTERS'
BY SATOSHI KANAZAWA AND ALAN MILLER

In Britain, 14.5m political conversations are held every day.
ELECTORAL COMMISSION

Mozart wrote a canon in B-flat major called 'Leck mich im
Arsch' (Lick My Arse).
WIKIPEDIA

Britons eat 97 per cent of the world's baked beans.
THE TIMES, 4TH OCTOBER 2007

Norman Mailer featured as the subject of *New Yorker* cartoons
eight times, but wrote for the magazine only five times.
EMDASHES, 12TH NOVEMBER 2007

On 2nd October 1995, Ireland lifted its 36-year ban on *Playboy*.

INDEX ON CENSORSHIP, VOLUME 24, ISSUE 6

Someone starting their first job in Britain in 2008 and buying their lunch every working day will spend an average £70,680 over their working lives.

THE GUARDIAN, 4TH FEBRUARY 2008

The average British person will, in the course of a lifetime, eat 550 poultry, 36 pigs, 36 sheep and eight cows.

PROSPECT, MAY 2001

Boy Scouts are not the most obvious symbols of political freedom. Yet *there is notable crossover between the six countries identified by Condoleezza Rice, the US secretary of state, as 'outposts of tyranny' in 2005 and the six countries that the BBC News website listed in 2007 as having no scouts.* Cuba, Burma and North Korea make both lists. Of the other three scoutless countries, China would almost certainly meet Rice's outpost test were it not effectively propping up the US economy, Laos is hardly a beacon of liberty and Andorra is too small to count. Scouting does, however, seem to be fairly robust in the three other outposts of tyranny – Belarus, Zimbabwe and Iran – suggesting that the freedom/ scouting relationship may have complex dimensions.

Only 20 per cent of Spaniards regularly have a siesta.

EL PAIS

Princess Anne has an HGV licence.

DAILY EXPRESS, 15TH AUGUST 2000

During George W Bush's state visit to Britain in late 2003, muggings in London went up by 20 per cent.

SCOTLAND YARD

Only 5 per cent of a mature tree's mass is alive.

'THE CLOCK OF THE LONG NOW' BY STEWART BRAND

The Sydney Olympic athletes' village was supplied with 752,000 condoms.

THE ECONOMIST, 15TH SEPTEMBER 2000

Only five out of every 100,000 paper clips are used to clip paper.

'THE BOOK OF GENERAL IGNORANCE'
BY JOHN MITCHINSON AND JOHN LLOYD

Red is the rarest shade of hair colour in existence. Britain and Ireland have a higher proportion of redheads than any other country.

THE GUARDIAN, 5TH JUNE 2007

Peanuts are used as an ingredient in dynamite.

THE TIMES OF INDIA, 2ND NOVEMBER 2003

St David is the only British patron saint who was born in the nation of which he is patron.

WIKIPEDIA

Scouting for Boys by Robert Baden-Powell was the fourth bestselling book of the 20th century across the world (after the Bible, the Koran and Mao's Little Red Book).

THE OBSERVER, 22ND APRIL 2007

One in ten adults has an extra pair of ribs.

VILLAGE VOICE, 17TH NOVEMBER 2003

Sheffield FC, formed on 24 October 1857, is officially
recognised by FIFA as the world's oldest football club.

BBC NEWS ONLINE, 24TH OCTOBER 2007

Six out of the top ten shoes on a 2007 police database of
footprints left at crime scenes were made by Nike.
(Three were Reebok and one Adidas.) Nike's Air Max
95 was the most popular; five out of the top six shoes
are Nike Air brands.

DAILY MIRROR, 27TH JUNE 2007

Subjects of the Roman empire had an average life expectancy
of 28 years.

NEW YORKER, 30TH APRIL 2007

The average pencil holds enough graphite to draw a line about
35 miles long, or to write roughly 45,000 words.

DISCOVER, MAY 2007

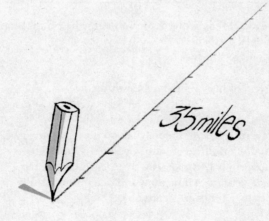

Over 90 days a single toad can consume nearly 10,000 insects.

ASHLEY MATTOON, STATE OF THE WORLD 2001, EARTHSCAN

The 7th July London bombings accounted for 7 per cent of all homicides in England and Wales in 2005–06.

HOME OFFICE

One of the many unexpected side-effects of climate change has been the growth of the English wine industry. For years the butt of oenophiles' jokes, English wine is now starting to be taken seriously as higher temperatures make it easier for the owners of Britain's 400 vineyards to cultivate a wider variety of grapes, and for more months of the year. In May 2007, the *Guardian* wrote that supermarkets were reporting *record growth in the sales of English wines*, and that a sparkling wine from England's largest vineyard had recently won a gold award in the International Wine Challenge, leading a record haul of 20 awards.

Enoch Powell sold his Wolverhampton home to a Caribbean couple.

THE OBSERVER, 24TH FEBRUARY 2008

Seven per cent of male zebra finches stutter.

NEW SCIENTIST, 23RD OCTOBER 1999

Three cast members from the 1987 action film *Predator* have run for the office of state governor in the US, two successfully (Arnold Schwarzenegger, California; Jesse Ventura, Minnesota) and one unsuccessfully (Sonny Landham, Kentucky).

WEEKLY STANDARD, 18TH AUGUST 2003

About 200 people around the world make a living by
designing typefaces.

THE ATLANTIC, JANUARY/FEBRUARY 2008

The average British woman spends two years of her life
gazing in the mirror.

THE TIMES, 7TH FEBRUARY 2007

40 per cent of bottled water sold by volume is tap water.

ECONOMIST.COM, 31ST JULY 2007

Almost 300 World Trade Centres exist; the World Trade
Centre Association licenses the name. In 2006
one opened in Hull.

FINANCIAL TIMES, 7TH SEPTEMBER 2007

Estonia spent its entire tourism budget for 2002 on hosting
the Eurovision song contest.

BBC NEWS ONLINE, 14TH MAY 2004

52 per cent of senior figures in the dairy industry believe that the
British government is actively anti-cheese.

THE TIMES, 2ND MAY 2007

To cover the £1.25m cost of his visit to Mexico in 1999, the
Pope had 25 official sponsors, including Pepsi.

THE INDEPENDENT, 23RD JANUARY 1999

Of the ten British constituencies with the highest
percentage of people saying they have no religion
at all, nine are in Scotland.

OFFICE FOR NATIONAL STATISTICS

Oxfam is Europe's biggest high street second-hand book retailer.

OXFAM

The 1968 Isle of Wight festival began as a fundraiser for a
local swimming pool association.

THE TIMES, 1ST JUNE 2002

At least 50,000 people have bought testicular implants for
their pets.

'DISCOVER YOUR INNER ECONOMIST' BY TYLER COWEN

The law allows you to kill or give away a bullfinch – but
not to sell or barter it.

'HOW TO LABEL A GOAT' BY ROSS CLARK

Since 1945, average height in Japan has increased by nearly
five inches.

TIMES LITERARY SUPPLEMENT, 25TH FEBRUARY 2005

The musical comedy You're a Good Man, Charlie Brown,
based on the comic strip *Peanuts*, went through
40,000 productions, involving 240,000 performers.

NEW YORKER, 22ND OCTOBER 2007

In Scotland, the most popular soft drink is Irn-Bru – making it
the only country in the world where neither Coca-Cola
nor Pepsi occupies the top spot.

BBC

Nasa has never had a space shuttle in the air over the transition
from 31st December to 1st January. It is not confident
about the onboard software coping with the switch.

LONDON REVIEW OF BOOKS, 6TH MARCH 2008

The fruit fly Drosophila bifurca is 1.5mm long, yet its sperm
are 6cm long.

NATURE, 6TH JULY 2000

Inheritance tax was invented by Emperor Augustus to raise
   funds for soldiers' pensions.

BBC NEWS MAGAZINE, 10TH OCTOBER 2007

The clitoris has 8,000 nerve fibres, which is more than the
   fingertips and tongue, and twice the number in
   the penis.

FINANCIAL TIMES, 24TH MARCH 2001

Hitler was on the shortlist for the 1938 Nobel Peace prize.

THE GUARDIAN, 7TH DECEMBER 2002

As of late 2007, the *New York Times* had 40 blogs.

GAWKER.COM

The Japanese consume almost a third of all the fish eaten
   in the world.

PROSPECT RESEARCH

The only major religion not to endorse abstinence from food
   on special occasions is Sikhism.

NEW YORKER, 3RD SEPTEMBER 2007

44 per cent of PhDs in biology and the life sciences are
   awarded to women.

EDGE.ORG

The number of children attending hospital emergency
   departments drops by almost half on the weekends
   when new Harry Potter books are published.

DAILY TELEGRAPH, 15TH JULY 2007

A cow burps up to 280 litres of methane per day.

THE GUARDIAN, 7TH JUNE 2001

The three most common requests by people planning their own funerals are to be cremated with their pet's ashes, to have a mobile phone in the coffin, and for someone to ensure that they are dead.

AGE CONCERN

An amputated newt limb will grow back fully within ten weeks.

CHRONICLE OF HIGHER EDUCATION, 31ST JANUARY 2003

Two thirds of the world's people have never seen snow.

CANADIAN WEATHER TRIVIA CALENDAR 2008

About 18 per cent of British men have had a vasectomy.

PROSPECT RESEARCH

Vladimir Nabokov spent seven years as a research fellow in entomology at Harvard.

'AT LARGE AND AT SMALL: CONFESSIONS OF A LITERARY HEDONIST'
BY ANNE FADIMAN

In 2003, there were just 15 professional ventriloquists left in Britain.

INDEPENDENT ON SUNDAY, 18TH MAY 2003

Windscreen wipers, laser printers and bullet-proof vests were all invented by women.

BRITISH ASSOCIATION FOR THE ADVANCEMENT OF SCIENCE

Every year, the world's deserts produce 1.7bn tonnes of dust.

BBC

Women spend nearly three years of their lives getting ready to leave the house. Men spend three months waiting for their wives and girlfriends while out shopping.

DAILY MAIL, 25TH NOVEMBER 2007

The economics of the music industry have been com-
pletely upended over the last ten years or so. While sales
of recorded music have slumped – the growth of the
legitimate download market pales in comparison to the
collapse in sales of CDs – live music has rarely been
stronger. Concerts by big names regularly sell out within days or even hours, the festival scene is flourishing,
particularly in Britain, and, most importantly for the
industry, ticket prices have skyrocketed. Writing about
the new dispensation in the August 2007 issue of *Prospect*,
Robert Sandall noted that *a decent seat at the Rolling
Stones's Twickenham gig in August 2006 would have set
you back at least £150. Back in 1990, the Stones took some
flak for charging a top price of £25 for their Wembley
concerts.* And while everyone from pub bands to chart-
toppers seems to be enjoying the boom in live music, it
seems to be middle-aged rockers from yesteryear who
are doing best of all; in late December 2007, the BBC
reported that *the Police had the highest earning music
tour in North America in 2007. The band's 54 gigs
generated $132m (£66m), almost double the total of
the second-placed act, country star Kenny Chesney.*

While filming Eyes Wide Shut, Stanley Kubrick shot 96 takes
of Tom Cruise walking through a door.

BBC RADIO 3

Woodrow Wilson is the only US president to have had a PhD.

WILSON CENTRE

In its first year of operation, the Serious Organised Crime
Agency's public hotline – manned five days a week –
received just 16 calls.

THE TIMES, 29TH NOVEMBER 2007

Since the formation of the solar system, 4.6bn years ago,
the sun has become 25–30 per cent hotter.

CARL SAGAN

As poet laureate, Andrew Motion is entitled to 'a butt of sack
per annum' – 110 gallons of Spanish sherry, or about
630 bottles, each year.

PROSPECT RESEARCH

The average bee produces one twelfth of a teaspoon of honey
during its lifetime.

HORIZONS, MARCH 2003

In the US, Muslims outnumber Jews.

ALI MAZRUI, RSA LECTURE

The Simon Wiesenthal Centre is still hunting 488 suspected
living Nazis.

HARPER'S, JANUARY 2008

Bacteria account for 10 per cent of our dry body weight.

CRISPIN TICKELL

In Britain, less than 1 per cent of death certificates list old age
as the cause of death.

'TIME OF OUR LIVES' BY TOM KIRKWOOD

The Wimbledon women finalists in 2001 – Venus Williams
(6'1") and Lindsay Davenport (6'2.5") – had a taller
combined height than the men.

PROSPECT RESEARCH

After Marilyn Monroe's death in 1962, the US suicide rate
increased temporarily by 12 per cent.

'THE TIPPING POINT' BY MALCOLM GLADWELL

Almost one in three of Britain's domestic rabbits is obese.

NATIONAL RABBIT WEEK 2008

Two thirds of Britons live within five miles of where they were
born and raised.

'THE NEW BARBARIAN MANIFESTO' BY IAN ANGELL

12 per cent of British men and 11 per cent of women meditate.

ROCHE/GALLUP POLL

In Japan, there is one vending machine for every 23 people.

JAPAN VENDING MACHINE MANUFACTURERS ASSOCIATION

There are more than 50,000 people in reading groups
in Britain.

OXFORD UNIVERSITY PRESS

Butterflies taste with their feet.

TORONTO STAR, 28TH MAY 2002

In Newfoundland, one in six people say they have had a
'ghost-rape' experience.

'SEX AND THE PARANORMAL' BY PAUL CHAMBERS

A man-sized rat could drink 12 bottles of scotch a day with no
more liver damage than a human would have from half
a bottle a day.

NATIONAL ANTI-VIVISECTION SOCIETY

95 per cent of filed documents remain filed for ever.

'FASTER' BY JAMES GLEICK

In 1997 and 1998, olive oil was the most adulterated agricultural
product in the EU, prompting the union's anti-fraud
office to establish an olive oil task force.

NEW YORKER, 13TH AUGUST 2007

Soon before he was sacked as England coach for failing to get his team into the 2008 European Championships, Steve McClaren attempted to pin the blame on the preponderance of foreign players in the Premier League. Just 38 per cent of players in the league were English, he said, making his job as coach of the national team next to impossible. While McClaren had his own reasons for identifying structural factors behind the decline of the English team, it's certainly true that the Premier League has become increasingly cosmopolitan during its relatively short life: according to the Professional Footballers Association, *back in 1992–93 over two thirds of top-flight players were English.* Now teams like Arsenal regularly field first teams without a single English player.

The most popular enquiry at Citizens Advice Bureaux concerns how to change one's name.

CITIZENS ADVICE BUREAUX

A garden worm has five pairs of hearts.

CORNELL UNIVERSITY

70 per cent of Land Rovers – first built in 1948 – are still on the road.

TOP GEAR

The Eiffel Tower is six inches taller in summer than in winter.

MICHELIN GREEN GUIDE

In the urban west, one out of three women has blonde hair; only one in 20 is blonde by nature.

'ON BLONDES' BY JOANNA PITMAN

Roughly 1 per cent of the static a detuned television receives
derives from the big bang.

'A SHORT HISTORY OF NEARLY EVERYTHING' BY BILL BRYSON

Henry David Thoreau once burnt down 300 acres of forest
trying to cook a fish he had caught for supper.

THE TIMES, 17TH APRIL 2003

Tony Blair was the first serving prime minister to send his
children to a state school.

'ON A CLEAR DAY' BY DAVID BLUNKETT

In New York City, January 2008 was the first essentially
snowless January in 75 years.

LIVESCIENCE, 30TH JANUARY 2008

Most toilets flush in E flat.

US CENTRES FOR DISEASE CONTROL AND PREVENTION

In the US, 64 per cent of gay people drink sparkling water,
compared to 17 per cent of all Americans.

'THE TELEVISION STUDIES READER'
EDITED BY ROBERT CLYDE ALLEN AND ANNETTE HILL

From 1901–2000, suicide rates were consistently lower under
Labour governments than Conservative.

JOURNAL OF EPIDEMIOLOGY AND COMMUNITY HEALTH, 2002

From a height of 3km it takes 30 minutes for a snowflake
to reach the ground.   CANADIAN WEATHER TRIVIA CALENDAR

In the US, abortions fell by 17 per cent throughout the 1990s,
reaching a 24-year low when George W Bush took
office in 2001. Then they started to rise again.

SOJOMAIL

A typical man is 50–70 per cent water; a typical woman 40–60 per cent.

ROCKY MOUNTAIN NEWS, 15TH APRIL 2003

Before a recent expansion, the Qatari national anthem lasted 32 seconds. The Greek national anthem has 158 verses.

NATIONAL-ANTHEMS.ORG

Most American car horns beep in F.

CHEVRONCARS.COM

On average, 1.2 second world war films are shown on television each day in Britain.

GOETHE-INSTITUT

Cristiano Ronaldo was named after Ronald Reagan.

UEFA EURO 2004 WEBSITE

On the day after George W Bush's re-election in 2004, Immigration Canada's website received a record 179,000 hits, with 64 per cent originating in the US.

BBC NEWS ONLINE

97 per cent of young Irish people have visited the United Kingdom.

'THROUGH IRISH EYES', BRITISH COUNCIL

One in five black people in the world is Nigerian.

RONDO IBERIA, JUNE 2004

More than 15 per cent of the British population owns a conservatory.

THE ECONOMIST, 5TH JUNE 2004

Mark Twain's *Life on the Mississippi* (1883) was the first
published novel to have been written on a typewriter.
The machine, a Sholes and Glidden, typed in capital
letters only.

EARTHLINK.NET

Stockport County FC owns 50 per cent of a Chinese team
called Stockport (formerly Liaoning) Tiger Star.

THE ECONOMIST, 14TH MAY 2004

In 2004, the average European man overtook the average
American in height for the first time since 1775.

BBC NEWS ONLINE, 14TH APRIL 2004

In 1377, 35 per cent of English men were named John.

THE OBSERVER, 14TH MARCH 2004

Peaches and almonds are both part of the rose family.

CANBERRA TIMES, 12TH MARCH 2000

On average, women take three times as long to use the toilet as men.

BRITISH TOILET ASSOCIATION

When India's Sachin Tendulkar bats against Pakistan in test matches, the television audience in India exceeds the total population of Europe.

THE OBSERVER, 11TH JANUARY 2004

General Motors' healthcare responsibilities make it the largest private purchaser of Viagra in the world. It spends $17m a year on the pills.

CONSUMERAFFAIRS.COM, 18TH APRIL 2006

50 per cent of speaking time consists of silence.

NEW YORK TIMES, 3RD JANUARY 2004

Tate Modern attracts over three times as many visitors as the Pompidou Centre.

THE GUARDIAN, 18TH OCTOBER 2005

Three quarters of all Oscar-winning films have been literary adaptations.

PROSPECT, MARCH 2003

In the 1930s, the Inland Revenue investigated Yeats's tax returns because they could not believe a poet of his stature had sales that were so small.

THE GUARDIAN, 13TH OCTOBER 2005

The human spine flexes 100m times in 50–60 years.

SYDNEY MORNING HERALD, 13TH OCTOBER 2005

There are more burglaries per head in Canada than in the US.

THE ECONOMIST, 1ST OCTOBER 2005

In 2004, the name David slipped out of the top 50 most popular names for newborn boys in Britain for the first time in over 60 years.

HORIZONS, JUNE 2005

The first edition of Freud's *The Interpretation of Dreams* (1899) sold only 351 copies in its first six years.

PROSPECT, OCTOBER 2005

Each successive monarch faces in a different direction on British coins.

BBC NEWS ONLINE

Seven of America's nine founding fathers denied the divinity of Jesus.

HARPER'S, JULY 2005

At birth, most babies cry at C or C-sharp.

FINANCIAL TIMES, 31ST JULY 2003

The penis of a barnacle may reach up to 20 times its body size.

THE INDEPENDENT, 27TH AUGUST 2004

British Muslims consume around a fifth of all lamb and mutton eaten in the country, despite making up just 3 per cent of the British population.

MUSLIM COUNCIL OF BRITAIN

One in every 3,400 Americans is an Elvis impersonator.

FINANCIAL TIMES, 7TH JUNE 2005

Queen Victoria spoke Urdu and Hindi.

THE GUARDIAN, 9TH NOVEMBER 2004

The average age of London's 25,000 cab drivers is 52, and there are more cabbies over 70 than there are under 30.

BLOOMBERG, 4TH OCTOBER 2007

Rats can run 100 yards in less than ten seconds and can jump six feet in the air.

DAILY MIRROR, 23RD AUGUST 2003

One American in 6,500 is injured by a toilet seat during their lifetime.

'THE PARANOID'S POCKET GUIDE' BY CAMERON TUTTLE

There are more people called Chang in China than there are people in Germany.

STEPHEN GREEN, CHAIRMAN, HSBC

Casanova spent the last 13 years of his life working as a librarian.

SUNDAY TIMES MAGAZINE, 23RD APRIL 2005

On average, redheads require 20 per cent more anaesthetic than people with differently coloured hair.

UNIVERSITY OF LOUISVILLE

A billion seconds ago, it was 1977. A billion minutes ago, Jesus had only recently died. A billion hours ago, our ancestors were living in the stone age.

SNOPES.COM

On a rough estimate, each newly conceived human has around 300 harmful genetic mutations.

EDGE.ORG

The idea of America as the 'new world' maintains a strong hold in the European consciousness, despite the fact that European settlement on the continent began well over 400 years ago. So here's a useful corrective for the next time you feel tempted to dismiss America's 'lack of history': *Galileo was offered a seat at Harvard University*, as reported in *The Right Nation*, John Micklethwait and Adrian Wooldridge's account of the rise of conservatism in the US. Harvard was founded in 1636; at the time Galileo was living under house arrest in his villa near Florence following his 1633 trial for heresy that resulted from his claim that the earth revolves around the sun. He was to die in 1642, so any career in Cambridge, Massachussetts, would probably have been short-lived, but it's still a salutary lesson in what we might call psychochronology.

Only two people have had their coffins transported on the London Underground: William Gladstone and Dr Barnardo.

WIKIPEDIA

London's Chinese population is the biggest of any city in Europe.

THE TIMES, 14TH FEBRUARY 2005

Men produce twice as much saliva as women.

PSYCHOLOGY TODAY, JULY/AUGUST 2003

Crematoria are responsible for up to 16 per cent of Britain's total mercury emissions.

THE OBSERVER, 20TH FEBRUARY 2006

Over 90 per cent of kebab shop sales are made after pub
closing hours.

RADIO 5 LIVE, 7TH FEBRUARY 2005

On average, ten cars a day emerging from English channel
crossings break down owing to the weight of duty-free
alcohol they carry.

'DRIVE ON', DSA, 2005

The most effective musical deterrents to loiterers and vandals
are anything sung by Pavarotti or written by Mozart.

THE ECONOMIST, 8TH JANUARY 2005

There are 2.5m pulped Mills and Boon books in the M6. The
paper's absorbency helps keep tarmac in place.

AUTO TRADER, 4TH DECEMBER 2007

41 per cent of British people stay at home every evening of the
week.

THE GUARDIAN, 8TH JANUARY 2005

In Britain, one woman in four prefers gardening to sex. The
numbers are highest in East Anglia, where the ratio is
one in three.

NEWEDEN

The Liechtensteinian national anthem has exactly the same
melody as 'God Save the Queen'.

RADIO 5 LIVE, 10TH SEPTEMBER 2003

On an average day, about 3.3 per cent of the world's population
has sex. Less than 0.4 per cent of these acts of
copulation results in a birth.

WORLD HEALTH ORGANISATION

Neither rabbits nor mice can vomit.

NATIONAL ANTI-VIVISECTION SOCIETY

In 2004, a survey found that 48 per cent of people in
Kensington and Chelsea lived alone.

SUNDAY TIMES, 24TH OCTOBER 2004

Just four bouquets of flowers were left outside Kensington
Palace in 2003 on the sixth anniversary of the death
of Diana, Princess of Wales.

THE INDEPENDENT, 9TH NOVEMBER 2003

Mitch Daniels, George W Bush's first budget director, tried
(and failed) to get the Office of Management and
Budget to use 'You Can't Always Get What You Want'
by the Rolling Stones as its hold music.

THE ECONOMIST, 4TH NOVEMBER 2006

Mozambique's flag features a Kalashnikov – the only gun to
appear on a national flag.

'THE GUN THAT CHANGED THE WORLD' BY MIKHAIL KALASHNIKOV

In the US there are more Mormons than Jews aged under 45.

PROSPECT, NOVEMBER 2006

6 per cent of all heart attacks occur during sexual intercourse.
Of these, 90 per cent happen during extramarital sex.

'THE GOLDEN AGE IS IN US' BY ALEXANDER COCKBURN

Half of British women own over 30 pairs of shoes.

THE GUARDIAN, 19TH AUGUST 2006

In any conversation lasting ten minutes or longer, 20 per cent
of adults will lie.

CALIFORNIA MAGAZINE, JULY/AUGUST 2007

The most expensive age of your life is 34.

THE GUARDIAN, 19TH AUGUST 2006

Five years after the 2001 terrorist attacks on New York and Washington, 1,248 books on 9/11 had been published.

THE INDEPENDENT, 11TH SEPTEMBER 2006

The gong struck at the beginning of Rank films was made out of papier mâché.

THE GUARDIAN, 19TH AUGUST 2006

The average Dutchman is 6 feet 1 inch tall, around four inches taller than British or American men.

MSNBC, 22ND JULY 2006

Jack Bauer, the lead character from the series *24*, personally killed 112 people in the first five seasons of the show.

THE GUARDIAN, 8TH JULY 2006

The only two people to have won both a Nobel prize and an Oscar are George Bernard Shaw and Al Gore.

THE INDEPENDENT, 13TH OCTOBER 2007

In 2003, in the week of National Poetry Day, poetry sales fell by 10 per cent compared to the previous week.

THE GUARDIAN, 18TH OCTOBER 2003

Aldous Huxley died on the same day JFK was assassinated in 1963.

NEW YORKER, 26TH JUNE 2006

Charles Dickens created 989 named characters.

THE GUARDIAN, 25TH MARCH 2006

Einstein did not learn to read until he was ten.

THE GUARDIAN, 6TH DECEMBER 2001

In Britain, more children are born to one white and one black parent than to two black parents.

THE ECONOMIST, 28TH OCTOBER 2006

On average, countries that win the World Cup add 0.7 per cent to their economic growth that year.

ABN AMRO

No Labour foreign secretary has ever officially visited Latin America.

COMMENT IS FREE, 15TH MAY 2006

Thomas Jefferson invented the swivel chair.

HOUSTON CHRONICLE, 18TH FEBRUARY 2006

The German band Tangerine Dream got their name from a
Blackpool FC nickname.

'THE BOOK OF LISTS: FOOTBALL' BY STEPHEN FOSTER

The average age of local councillors in Britain is 58. 87 per cent
of councillors are over 45.

COUNCILLORS' CENSUS, 2006

10 per cent of people are left-handed and 20 per cent
left-footed.

'RIGHT HAND, LEFT HAND' BY CHRIS MCMANUS

Starbucks bought 37 per cent of Costa Rica's entire coffee crop
in the 2004–05 season.

THE ECONOMIST, 1ST APRIL 2006

In 2003, John Irving, a practising Muslim and twin brother of
historian and convicted Holocaust denier David Irving,
was appointed chairman of the Wiltshire racial equality
council.

PROSPECT RESEARCH

The philosopher Daniel Dennett introduced the frisbee to
Britain.

THE OBSERVER, 12TH MARCH 2006

The average age of the first-time grandparent in Britain is 49.

DAILY TELEGRAPH, 28TH JULY 2005

In Britain, those born in September have a 20 per cent better
chance of entering higher education aged 18 than those
born in August.

HEFCE

One in four British households owns a copy of Pink Floyd's
   Dark Side of the Moon.
                                    THE GUARDIAN, 3RD MARCH 2006

Senegal's only athlete at the 2006 Winter Olympics, Leyti Seck,
   competing as an alpine skier, was brought up in Austria
   and had never been to Senegal.
                                                      REUTERS

The Coca-Cola brand is estimated to be worth $67bn, making
   it the most valuable in the world.
                                          B2B INTERNATIONAL

Ruth Kelly's grandfather was an IRA quartermaster.
                                    THE TIMES, 23RD JANUARY 2006

One in three men of Bangladeshi origin in Britain works as a
   waiter, and one in eight Pakistanis as a taxi driver.
                      DAVID MILIBAND'S SCARMAN LECTURE, 31ST JANUARY 2006

95 per cent of all patent applications in the US are approved,
   compared with just 65 per cent in Europe and Japan.
                                    NEW YORKER, 26TH DECEMBER 2005

The following events in German history all took place on 9th
   November: the abdication of the kaiser and the
   proclamation of the Republic (1918), the failure of
   the Munich beer-hall putsch (1923), Kristallnacht (1938)
   and the fall of the Berlin wall (1989).
                                              THE VIRTUAL STOA

If all the Lego in the world were divided up evenly, we would
   get 30 pieces each.
                            'DAD STUFF' BY STEVE CAPLIN AND SIMON ROSE

The philosopher René Descartes (1596–1650) was a dualist; he believed the mind and body to be distinctly different substances, and claimed that while we cannot deny the existence of the former, the latter is open to doubt. But despite this body-scepticism – or perhaps because of it – Descartes was something of a hypochondriac. *Richard Watson, in his 2002 biography of Descartes, claimed that the philosopher was so afraid of the plague that he moved house around 18 times in 21 years.* In 1649 he was summoned to Sweden by the young Queen Christina, who wanted him to tutor her in philosophy. Unused to the cold weather forced upon him by Christina's early morning regime, Descartes contracted pneumonia and died shortly afterwards.

George Bernard Shaw, Laurence Olivier, Prince Charles and John Prescott all declined invitations to appear on *Desert Island Discs*.

SUNDAY TIMES, 2ND JULY 2006

Ali Daei is the all-time top goalscorer in international football. In his 148 appearances for Iran until his retirement in 2007, he scored 109 times.

FIFA

Research on guinea pigs has resulted in 23 Nobel prizes.

'A GUINEA PIG'S HISTORY OF BIOLOGY' BY JIM ENDERSBY

Deutsche Bank employs more people in London than in Frankfurt.

NEW STATESMAN, 19TH JULY 2007

80 per cent of admissions to hospital are for emergencies.

THE GUARDIAN, 3RD FEBRUARY 2006

Romania has had six different national anthems since the second world war.

WALL STREET JOURNAL, 17TH MAY 2002

Eleven out of the 12 men to have walked on the moon were in the Boy Scouts.

BOY SCOUTS OF AMERICA NATIONAL COUNCIL

Women who receive implants for breast enhancement are three times more likely to commit suicide than other women.

LOS ANGELES TIMES, 8TH AUGUST 2007

It takes 100 years for the deep-sea clam to grow to the length of a third of an inch.

'THE BOOK OF USELESS INFORMATION'
BY KEITH WATERHOUSE AND RICHARD LITTLEJOHN

Isaac Newton invented the cat flap.

SCIENCE MUSEUM

Elgar is the only major composer to have mastered the bassoon.

THE SPECTATOR, 9TH JUNE 2007

The going rate for the tooth fairy in Britain is £1.05, compared to 17p in 2002. During this period the price of teeth has risen over three times as quickly as the cost of living.

DAILY TELEGRAPH, 27TH JUNE 2007

About 70 per cent of Chinese students who leave to study abroad don't return.

RICHARD SPENCER, DAILY TELEGRAPH BLOG, 15TH JUNE 2007

New Zealanders visit the cinema an average of eight times a
year – more than anyone else. The British make about
three visits; Indians just one and a half.

ECONOMIST.COM, 31ST MAY 2007

Scotland has the highest proportion of redheads in the world:
13 per cent of Scots have red hair and 40 per cent carry
the recessive ginger gene.

THE OBSERVER, 8TH JULY 2007

In Britain, 1.3 per cent of lorry drivers are female and 2 per cent
from ethnic minorities.

BBC NEWS, 3RD JULY 2007

The new Wembley stadium has 2,600 toilets – more than any
building in the world.

EVENING STANDARD, 1ST MAY 2007

At 0.6 miles an hour, the London Eye moves twice as fast as a
sprinting tortoise.

LONDON EYE WEBSITE

Most telephones have dial tones in the key of F.

'THE BOOK OF USELESS INFORMATION'
BY KEITH WATERHOUSE AND RICHARD LITTLEJOHN

Half the world's population has seen at least one of the 17
James Bond films.

PENGUIN

Those who eat with one other person consume about 35 per
cent more than when they are alone; members of a
group of four eat about 75 per cent more; those in
groups of seven or more eat 96 per cent more.

NEW REPUBLIC, 22ND MARCH 2007

In its first year, 1903, Gillette sold just 51 razors and 168 blades.

WIRED, 16TH MARCH 2008

A female ferret will die if it goes into heat and cannot find a mate.

FERRETSMAGAZINE.COM

The happiness boost that men gain from a firstborn son is 75 per cent larger than from a firstborn daughter. Second and third children don't add to the happiness of either parent.

PSYCHOLOGY TODAY, 12TH APRIL 2007

Italy and Saudi Arabia were the only two teams in the 2006 World Cup whose squads were entirely home-based.

BBCI

In 2005, the number of British women worth £200,000 or more (448,100) overtook the number of men (429,300).

NEW ZEALAND HERALD, 28TH APRIL 2007

The closest living relative of the tyrannosaurus rex is the chicken.

THE GUARDIAN, 13TH APRIL 2007

Since 1961, 40 US senators have run for president. Every one has failed. But both major candidates in the 2008 presidential election are senators.

NEW YORK TIMES, 4TH MARCH 2007/PROSPECT RESEARCH

IBM once sold a cheap printer, LaserWriterE, which was exactly the same model as the pricier LaserWriter except that it had a chip installed to slow it down.

'THE UNDERCOVER ECONOMIST' BY TIM HARFORD

American Airlines once saved $1m by removing a single olive
from each salad served in first class.

THE BUSINESS, 11TH–12TH MAY 2001

Napoleon was actually 5 feet 6.5 inches; taller than the
average early 19th-century Frenchman.

THE OBSERVER, 25TH MARCH 2007

The 6.5bn people alive today make up about 6 per cent of the
number of people who have ever been born.

SCIENTIFIC AMERICAN, 1ST MARCH 2007

The bestselling work of fiction in the US in 1977 was
The Silmarillion, by JRR Tolkien.

PROSPECT, JANUARY 2007

The top 100 bestselling albums in British history include no
Rolling Stones, Bob Dylan or Sex Pistols.

THE GUARDIAN, 16TH NOVEMBER 2006

Adjusting for inflation, the most expensive film ever made is the
1963 version of *Cleopatra*, which cost almost $300m in
2006 money.

NEW YORKER, 8TH JANUARY 2007

Donald Rumsfeld, who served in both the Nixon and George
W Bush cabinets, is both the youngest and the oldest
defence secretary in US history.

BBC NEWS ONLINE, 28TH DECEMBER 2006

Of the arms deliveries to Iraq between 1973 and 2002, 57 per
cent came from the Soviet Union, 13 per cent from
France, 12 per cent from China, 0.5 per cent from the
US and 0.2 per cent from Britain.

'WHAT'S LEFT?' BY NICK COHEN

Reviews on amazon.com give an average 4.2 stars out of five.

SMARTMONEY.COM

Israelis own 10 per cent of the private land on the moon.

JERUSALEM POST, 4TH JANUARY 2007

Gordon Brown is the first university-educated prime minister since Stanley Baldwin not to attend Oxford.

SUTTON TRUST

Franz Liszt received so many requests for a lock of his hair that he bought a dog and snipped off patches of fur to send to his admirers.

'CONDENSED KNOWLEDGE: A DELICIOUSLY IRREVERENT GUIDE TO FEELING SMART AGAIN'

The management of Joseph Lyons, of tea house fame, built
their own computer and thus became one of the
first companies to use computers in business.

PROSPECT RESEARCH

The average male orgasm lasts for eight seconds; the average
female orgasm 20 seconds.

THE OBSERVER, 11TH FEBRUARY 2001

Americans use less water per head today than 25 years ago.

NEW YORKER, 23RD OCTOBER 2006

48 per cent of landlines in Britain are ex-directory.

BBC NEWS MAGAZINE, 14TH SEPTEMBER 2006

The record for the highest number of short stories published in
the *New Yorker* by an author in one year is held by EB
White (28 in 1927). The overall record is held by James
Thurber, who published 273 stories from 1927–61.

EMDASHES, 16TH OCTOBER 2006

There are more than 400 escalators on the London
Underground.

LONDONIST.COM, 17TH MARCH 2008

62 of the world's 100 richest men are married to brunettes,
22 to blondes, 16 to 'raven-haired' women, and none
to a redhead.

LYCOS

No English manager has ever won the Premier League.

WIKIPEDIA

The 'close doors' button doesn't work in most lifts.

NEW YORKER, 21ST APRIL 2008

Science fiction writer Ray Bradbury avoids computers and ATMs and claims he has never driven a car. Isaac Asimov refused to board an aeroplane.

DISCOVER, 30TH JANUARY 2008

Bill Gates gets 4m emails a day.

NEW STATESMAN, 25TH JANUARY 2007

In Britain, each month from May 2007 to April 2008 was cooler than the month 12 months before.

RADIO 5 LIVE, 5TH MAY 2008

There are 109 journeys between London's Tube stations that are quicker to walk.

BBC

To help break the champagne when a new ship is launched, P&O sometimes scores the bottle with a glass-cutter.

BBC

No Chinese national has won a Nobel prize.

PROSPECT RESEARCH

The metal value of some US pennies exceeds their face value. A penny minted before 1982 is 95 per cent copper. At recent prices, this is worth about two and a half cents.

NEW YORKER, 31ST MARCH 2008

The world's first PC was a Honeywell kitchen appliance, produced in 1969, with integrated counter space.

WIRED, 16TH MARCH 2008

In Britain, trousers cause twice as many accidents as chainsaws.

BRITISH COUNCIL

IN PERSPECTIVE

Facts that shift the tectonic plates
of your thinking

About 80 per cent of all news on the internet originates from print newspapers.

NEW YORK REVIEW OF BOOKS, 16TH AUGUST 2007

Assuming that only 10 per cent of the oil in the tar sands of Alberta, Canada, is recoverable, it still represents the second largest reserve in the world after Saudi Arabia – more than Kuwait, Norway and Russia combined.

NEW YORKER, 12TH NOVEMBER 2007

In 2003, American companies invested twice as much in Ireland as they did in China.

FOREIGN POLICY, SEPTEMBER/OCTOBER 2005

China won 63 medals at the 2004 Olympics, 32 of them gold. India won just one: a silver in shooting.

PROSPECT, DECEMBER 2007

Half the people living near Heathrow support the opening of a third runway.

BBC NEWS ONLINE, 8TH OCTOBER 2007

In 2005, on average, fewer than 16 people a week used the 800 smallest rural post offices in Britain, costing the taxpayer £17 per visit.

DEPARTMENT FOR BUSINESS, ENTERPRISE AND REGULATORY REFORM

The top 25 hedge fund managers in the US earn more than the CEOs of the S&P 500 companies combined.

MARGINAL REVOLUTION, 22ND JULY 2007

More explosive power was dropped on Serbia in 1999 than during the entire Vietnam war.

ROBERT FOX

More than 80 per cent of new global oil reserves discovered between 2001 and 2004 were in west Africa.

LONDON REVIEW OF BOOKS, 5TH JULY 2007

As of early 2007, the death rate in Zimbabwe was greater than that in Darfur.

NEW REPUBLIC, 8TH MARCH 2007

In 1820, Asia accounted for 56 per cent of world output. In 1900 the Asian economies accounted for about 32 per cent of world output. Today it is just over a third.

PROSPECT RESEARCH

America's prison population is higher than China's.

CROOKED TIMBER

More people die as a result of dog attacks in the US each year than have been killed by sharks in the last 100 years.

SUNDAY TELEGRAPH, 5TH AUGUST 2007

Everyone knows that computer games are big business – by some measures, far bigger business than movies. But it may still come as a surprise to read that the MMORPG ('massively multiplayer online role-playing game') **World of Warcraft *had, by early 2006, more than twice as many players in the US (4m) as the country had farmers (2m)*,** a comparison made by the blog 'Kung Fu Monkey'. Presumably a good number of those *World of Warcraft* players make a 'living' from agriculture, growing the 'food' needed to sustain the world's inhabitants. So if the game continues to grow and real-world agriculture in the US to decline, it's possible to imagine a future where there are more virtual farmers in America than real ones.

Now that the debate over whether climate change is caused by humans or not is largely resolved, closer attention is being paid to those aspects of human behaviour that contribute to global warming – with sometimes surprising results. In July 2007, the *New Scientist* reported that ***the production of a kilogram of beef emits the same amount of carbon dioxide as the average European car driving 250 kilometres.*** We are only just beginning to think about how climate change might force us to change the way we eat, but when it seems increasingly clear that a diet heavy in meat significantly increases our carbon footprint, one can start to imagine that in the near future, eating a hamburger may be considered as much of an eco-sin as driving a 4x4 in the city.

It typically costs 12p to send a 160-character text message from one British mobile phone to another. Byte for byte, this works out as over 12 times what Nasa pays to retrieve data from the Hubble Space Telescope.

THE INDEPENDENT, 1ST AUGUST 2007

Global newspaper sales have risen by over 9 per cent in the past five years.

THE OBSERVER, 10TH JUNE 2007

The US navy is as large as the next 17 navies in the world combined.

INTERNATIONAL HERALD TRIBUNE, 8TH AUGUST 2007

In 2003, the World Trade Organisation's budget was less than a quarter of the World Wide Fund for Nature's.

FOREIGN POLICY, JANUARY/FEBRUARY 2003

British charities received £8.9bn from individuals in voluntary
    donations in 2005–06 – exactly the same amount as was
    paid out in City bonuses.

BBC NEWS ONLINE, 12TH JULY 2007

There are more Arabs in Brazil than in the Palestinian
    territories.

WASHINGTON POST, 19TH NOVEMBER 2007

The money transfer company Western Union has as many
    outlets worldwide as McDonald's, Starbucks, Burger
    King and Wal-Mart combined.

NEW YORK TIMES, 22ND NOVEMBER 2007

2008 is the first year in which China has spent more than
    Britain on defence, according to official figures.

PROSPECT RESEARCH

One of the more distasteful aspects of American politics
is its ready slide into economic populism; rants against
free trade agreements, globalisation, migrant labour and
so forth. On top of the latent xenophobia that sometimes
seems to underlie such sentiments, you often find that
they are based on a rather selective reading of the facts.
Take labour outsourcing, a common target of the economic populist. In 2004, *Daniel Drezner wrote in Foreign Affairs that in the US, between 1983 and 2000, the
number of outsourced jobs increased by slightly over half,
from 6.5m to 10m. Meanwhile, the number of 'insourced'
jobs – jobs outsourced to the US by other countries – rose
more than two and a half times, from 2.5m to 6.5m.* In
other words, while an increasing number of jobs are being shipped abroad from the US, jobs are being imported
at an even faster rate.

In 2006, data centres in the US consumed more power than televisions.

HARPER'S, MARCH 2008

Between 1969 and 2002, a citizen of Northern Ireland was over 200 times more likely to die from sectarian violence than a citizen of India.

PROSPECT, MAY 2002

There are 40,000 Chinese restaurants in the US – more than the number of McDonald's, Burger Kings and KFCs combined.

'THE FORTUNE COOKIE CHRONICLES: ADVENTURES IN THE WORLD OF CHINESE FOOD' BY JENNIFER 8 LEE

There are 123,598,000 Muslims living in India – only slightly fewer than the 140,277,000 who live in Pakistan.

CIA

In the US, more bachelor's degrees are awarded every year in parks, recreation, leisure and fitness studies than in all foreign languages and literatures combined.

NEW YORKER, 21ST MAY 2007

China produces less than 4 per cent of the world's exports; India less than 1 per cent.

'THE UNDERCOVER ECONOMIST' BY TIM HARFORD

A typical Hewlett-Packard inkjet printer cartridge costs £29 for 17ml, or £1.70 per ml, compared with Dom Pérignon 1985 vintage champagne, which costs 23p per ml.

WHICH?

In 2002, there were 199 terrorist incidents recorded worldwide – the lowest total since 1969.

US STATE DEPARTMENT

The policy implications of health economics are full of awkward trade-offs and uncomfortable dilemmas. Consider the fact that plenty of us believe that people who voluntarily endanger their health – through dangerous sports, smoking and so on – should bear some of the responsibility for the higher healthcare costs they tend to incur. Indeed, this is one of the justifications for the high rates of taxation applied to cigarettes and alcohol. But if we take this view, are we not also obliged to 'reward' such groups for the fact that their voluntary activities are, on average, liable to shorten their lifespan, thus relieving the public purse? This is not idle philosophising: in February 2008, the *Daily Telegraph* reported that *an average person of normal weight incurred healthcare costs of £210,000 over their lifetime, an obese person £187,000 and a smoker just £165,000.*

The US economy grows as much in a day as it did in a year in the 1930s.

SPECIALIST SCHOOLS TRUST

There are more atoms in a glass of water than glasses of water in all the oceans in the world.

SCIENCE YOU CAN'T SEE: THE ATOM, BBC4

Every week, ten times more people in China watch Premier League football than in Britain.

THE GUARDIAN, 19TH JANUARY 2008

Over a fifth of the members of Pakistan's parliament are women – compared to 17 per cent of members of the US congress.

INTER-PARLIAMENTARY UNION

The conflict between Israel and the Palestinians encompasses all the most potent issues of modern geopolitics: terrorism, religion, colonialism. Events in the region are followed more closely than almost anywhere else in the world, and everyone has a view on the situation. That's why it can be useful to remind yourself that the disputed territory is absolutely tiny. *At 365 square km, the Gaza strip is slightly smaller than Sheffield. As for the West Bank, it's roughly the same size as Lincolnshire: 6,000 square km.* Israel itself is a behemoth by comparison – its 20,000 square km make it just a bit smaller than Wales.

In 2003, Britain was responsible for 2.9 per cent of global oil production, slightly less than Kuwait's 3.0 per cent.

THE ECONOMIST, 7TH NOVEMBER 2004

Until the fall of Edward Shevardnadze in 2003, US per capita aid to Georgia was higher than to any other country in the world bar Israel.

THE NATION, 16TH FEBRUARY 2004

The annual budget of the World Health Organisation is $1.65bn. Between 2000 and 2005, the (Bill and Melinda) Gates Foundation spent $6bn on health issues in the third world.

NEW YORKER, 24TH OCTOBER 2005

Jon Corzine spent more on winning his New Jersey Senate seat in 2000 than the total spend of every political party in the British general election of 2001.

NEW YORK REVIEW OF BOOKS, 15TH MAY 2003

Only 16 per cent of Germans hold a university degree; about the same proportion as Turkey and Mexico.

OECD

In 2004, GDP per head in the EU as a whole was higher than only Arkansas, Montana, West Virginia and Mississippi among the 50 US states.

NEW YORK TIMES, 17TH APRIL 2005

New York City's police force is nearly four times bigger than America's entire border patrol.

THE ECONOMIST, 1ST APRIL 2006

In China and Japan, 59 per cent and 66 per cent of undergraduates respectively receive their degrees in science and engineering, compared with 32 per cent in the US.

WASHINGTON POST, 6TH DECEMBER 2006

In 2002, more people travelled by train in one day in India than by plane in an entire year.

SHASHI THAROOR

58,000 Britons still have a black and white television.

THE TIMES, 25TH NOVEMBER 2005

Between 1948 and 1998, 20,362 Israelis were killed in the wars with neighbouring states, and 20,852 were killed on the roads.

JERUSALEM REPORT, 22ND NOVEMBER 1999

Oslo is about the same distance from Rome as it is from the northernmost point of the Norwegian land mass.

PROSPECT RESEARCH

35 per cent of Turks say they believe their country is 'governed according to the will of the people', more than Britain (30 per cent), France (26) or Germany (18).

VOICE OF THE PEOPLE SURVEY 2006

Roughly 11,000 British people live full-time in the Palestinian territories.

IPPR

The World Bank's lending to Africa from July 2006 to April 2007 was \$1bn lower than the same period a year earlier.

NEW YORKER, 9TH APRIL 2007

For several years, the annual expansion in China's trade has been larger than India's total annual trade.

VOXEU.ORG

Asians make up 35 per cent of the undergraduate body at MIT, but only 4 per cent of the US population.

NEW YORK REVIEW OF BOOKS, 3RD NOVEMBER 2005

The Amazon river's course is 3,900 miles, the distance from New York to Rome.

INTERNATIONAL HERALD TRIBUNE, 21ST DECEMBER 2000

Canada has over 200,000 km of coastline – almost four times as much as the country behind, Indonesia, with around 58,000 km.

CIA FACTBOOK

In welfare services and healthcare in Britain, people aged over 85 cost 15 times as much per head as people aged 5–64.

'THE FUTURE OF BRITAIN AND EUROPE', POLICY STUDIES INSTITUTE

It is tempting to think of online activities as clean and 'weightless', to assume that their virtual nature means they can have no direct impact upon the physical world – and in particular, no deleterious effects upon the environment. But the truth is a bit more complicated. Aside from all the dirty manufacturing work that goes into the production of computers, networking infra-structure and so on, those machines helping us weightlessly communicate with each other consume an awful lot of power. In late 2006, the blog Rough Type calculated that *an average 'avatar' (character) in the virtual reality world* Second Life *is responsible for the consumption of roughly the same amount of electricity per year as a typical Brazilian*, given the number of servers required by *Second Life*'s 'owners', Linden Lab, to keep the world going.

Indians use 73kg of fertilisers on a hectare of cropland; Germans use 500.

ROWLAND MORGAN

London has 13 per cent of Britain's population, but just 9 per cent of its pubs.

LONDONIST.COM, 20TH AUGUST 2007

The average American two-car garage is 25 per cent bigger than the average Tokyo home.

'FAT, DUMB AND UGLY' BY PETER STRUPP

While London's domestic gardens take up only a fifth of the capital's surface area, they contain nearly 70 per cent of its 5.5m trees.

PROSPECT, APRIL 2005

Britain is notorious for locking people up: the imprison-
ment rate for England and Wales stands at 149 per
100,000 population – the highest figure in western
Europe bar Luxembourg – and prison numbers have
risen 60 per cent since 1995. Yet look at the numbers a
different way, in terms of the number of imprisonments
per crime committed, and we start to look almost like
a soft touch: *in England and Wales, 12 people are im-
prisoned for every 1,000 crimes committed. In Ireland
the figure is 33 per 1,000; in Spain it is 48 per 1,000.*
(The figures are from the *Independent*, February 2007.)

On one day in 2005, *Harry Potter and the Half-Blood Prince* sold
more copies than did Dan Brown's *The Da Vinci Code*
the whole year.
THE INDEPENDENT, 10TH JUNE 2007

In 2003 in the US, power generation companies spent less on
R&D than pet food companies did.
THE ECONOMIST, 2ND JUNE 2007

Russian GDP is still only at around 85 per cent of its 1989
figure.
NEW LEFT REVIEW, MARCH/APRIL 2007

More British servicemen and women have committed suicide
over the past two decades than have died in military
action.
THE INDEPENDENT, 1ST APRIL 2007

Per capita, Cuba grants more patents than either China
or India.
ECONOMIST.COM, 30TH JULY 2007

Since Ted Heath and until David Cameron, every Tory leader apart from Iain Duncan Smith has been state-educated.

NEW REPUBLIC, 2ND DECEMBER 2005

Canada supplies the US with more oil than all the Gulf nations put together.

NEW YORKER, 12TH NOVEMBER 2007

Per capita, there are more psychoanalysts in Buenos Aires than anywhere in the world.

DAILY TELEGRAPH, 14TH JANUARY 2006

Britain and France, followed by the US and Russia/USSR, have fought the most international wars since 1946.

HUMAN SECURITY REPORT 2005

The EU exports more to Switzerland than to China.

WALL STREET JOURNAL, 12TH JUNE 2007

In the second world war, 1.8 per cent of Americans enrolled in the services were killed in action. In Vietnam that figure dropped to 0.6 per cent and in the Gulf war to just 0.005 per cent.

PROSPECT, APRIL 2003

Three times as much money is invested by rich Africans in foreign bank accounts than is sent to the continent as remittances by overseas African workers.

PROSPECT, FEBRUARY 2006

Mongolia has roughly the same population as Wales.

THE GUARDIAN, 21ST NOVEMBER 2005

Per capita, Sudan has more rainfall than Britain.

DAILY TELEGRAPH, 2ND MARCH 2006

The average British mother spent the same time on childcare
in 2003 as in 1965.

THE ECONOMIST, 15TH APRIL 2006

China is the third largest international food donor in the world,
largely because of its cereal shipments to North Korea.

FINANCIAL TIMES, 20TH JULY 2006

The Exxon Valdez oil spill killed 250,000 birds. This is
approximately the same number that die colliding with
plate glass every day in the US.

PROSPECT, OCTOBER 2001

Of the trillions of cells in a typical human body, only about one
in ten is human. The rest are microbial.

NEW YORK TIMES MAGAZINE, 13TH AUGUST 2006

Ever since *Jaws* seared a deep fear of killer great whites
into the collective consciousness back in 1975, conserva-
tion groups concerned about dwindling numbers of some
species of shark have struggled to convince a wary public
that fears of attack are wildly overdone. Peter Benchley
himself, author of the novel that Spielberg's film was
based on, later expressed regret for the way his book
had misrepresented sharks. *Jaws* does indeed have a lot
to answer for, as the chances of being killed by a shark are
minuscule. In June 2007, the *Guardian* reported that *in
the US, just 12 people have been killed by shark attacks
since 1990. This makes sharks responsible for four fewer
fatalities than holes dug in the sand to make sandcastles.*
So next time you're at the beach, you know what to
watch out for.

If, as Auguste Comte wrote, demography is destiny, Israel has a problem on its hands. The birth rate in the occupied Palestinian territories is far higher than in Israel itself; on current trends, by 2020 Palestinians in the West Bank, Gaza and East Jerusalem along with Israeli Arabs will outnumber Israeli Jews. *Even in Jerusalem, the supposed 'eternal capital' of the Jewish state, the Arab population has grown twice as fast as the Jewish over the past decade*, according to an *AFP* report in May 2007. Noting the trend, some Palestinians now argue that rather than pressing for an independent Palestine, they should seek the formation of a single democratic binational state, taking in Israel and the occupied territories, in which Arabs and Jews would have equal rights. When Tony Judt, a US-based Jewish historian, made a similar proposition in an article for the *New York Review of Books* in 2003, he attracted huge criticism and was apparently removed from the editorial board of the *New Republic*.

Without the black vote, the Democrats would have won the US presidency only once, in 1964.

THE GUARDIAN, 18TH SEPTEMBER 2006

In the US, tobacco kills nearly half a million people annually; more than HIV, alcohol, illegal drugs, suicide and homicide combined.

TIMES LITERARY SUPPLEMENT, 28TH SEPTEMBER 2007

More slave labourers died building the V2 rocket than were ever killed by it.

'THE SHOCK OF THE NEW' BY DAVID EDGERTON

The explosion in cheap flights over the past ten years or so means that aviation is now the fastest-growing source of Britain's carbon dioxide emissions. So it's hardly surprising that many campaigners argue that we will have to break our love affair with the aeroplane if we are to meet our environmental obligations. Yet some have claimed to see in such arguments a new snobbery, in which wealthy elites adopt the guise of environmentalism in order to keep the plebs off planes and reserve the luxuries of flying to themselves. But a point perhaps missed by both sides is that flying is nothing like as egalitarian a pursuit as we are often led to believe. In August 2007, the *New Statesman* reported that *a third of return flights from Britain in 2006 were made by just 4 per cent of the population.* And even more revealingly, over half the population took no flights at all.

Pneumonia kills more children worldwide than any other illness – and more than AIDS, malaria and measles combined.

UNICEF

In the US in the 20th century, five times more people were killed in traffic accidents than died in war. Total fatalities on the road up until 1997 were 2.98m, compared with war deaths totalling 605,000.

PROSPECT RESEARCH

Around 2.4 per cent of the world's population was killed in the second world war and 0.5 per cent in the first, compared with 0.2 in the Napoleonic wars.

'THE CASH NEXUS' BY NIALL FERGUSON

The secular Tamil Tigers in Sri Lanka are responsible for more
suicide bombings than any other terrorist organisation
in the world – up to two thirds of the total committed.

PBS

Only 4 per cent of US films are made by women, compared to
25 per cent in Iran.

THE OBSERVER, 18TH JANUARY 2004

Every day, 44,000 babies are born in China – roughly the
population of Canterbury.

PROSPECT RESEARCH

In 2007, an average piece of chewing gum cost 3p, while the
average cost of removing it from a street or pavement
was 10p.

THE GUARDIAN, 3RD MAY 2008

At any moment, there are almost twice as many chickens alive
as humans.

'PLANET CHICKEN' BY HATTIE ELLIS

There are 731 crimes in Glasgow for every 100,000 people, compared to 631 in New York.

REFORM SCOTLAND REPORT

Britain is the world's fifth biggest manufacturer.

BBC NEWS, 4TH APRIL 2008

Iran's population is only 51 per cent Persian.

LOS ANGELES TIMES, 25TH OCTOBER 2006

Police officers in Los Angeles are more likely to take their own life than be killed by a criminal. 19 Los Angeles police officers killed themselves between 1998 and 2007, while only seven died in the line of duty.

LOS ANGELES TIMES, 26TH MARCH 2008

BE VERY
Afraid

Facts to make you want to stay in bed

Africa has less than 4 per cent of the world's air traffic, but one third of its air disasters. Around two thirds of the airlines banned by the EU on safety grounds are African.

MONOCLE, MAY 2007

Facial herpes – or 'scrum pox' – is common among the forwards in a rugby team.

STUDENTHEALTH.CO.UK

In 2005–06, 24 virginity repair operations were carried out on the NHS.

EVENING STANDARD, 15TH NOVEMBER 2007

Most babies in Britain are conceived without the conscious consent of the father.

IPPR

The US – with 5 per cent of the world's population – houses 25 per cent of the world's prison inmates. Its incarceration rate (714 per 100,000 residents) is almost 40 per cent greater than those of the nearest competitors (the Bahamas, Belarus and Russia).

BOSTON REVIEW, JULY/AUGUST 2007

The US government's terrorist watch list contains around 755,000 names.

CNN, 25TH OCTOBER 2007

In late 2007, there were five people under 18 in custody in Finland. In Britain there were roughly 3,000. If the populations of the two countries were equal, Britain would have had 60 in custody at Finnish levels.

PROSPECT RESEARCH

Greeks smoke an average 3,000 cigarettes a year.

ECONOMIST.COM, 15TH MAY 2007

The cost of a coffin in Baghdad is $50–75, up from $5–10 before the Iraq war.

WASHINGTON POST, 18TH NOVEMBER 2007

You could fit all the surviving members of the 25 most endangered species of primates in one (US) football stadium.

NEW YORK TIMES, 27TH OCTOBER 2007

There are 67m rats in Britain – 1.2 for every person.

BBCI

10 per cent of the flow of the Yellow river is raw sewage.

INSTITUTE OF PUBLIC AND ENVIRONMENTAL AFFAIRS

The formal definition of hyperinflation is sometimes taken to be monthly price rises of over 50 per cent. But in the early 1990s, Yugoslavia had it a lot worse than that. The journal *East European Politics and Societies* reported that *between October 1993 and January 1995, prices in Yugoslavia increased by five quadrillion per cent. This is a 5 with 15 zeros after it.* Some economists claim this to be the worst episode of hyperinflation in history. Yugoslavia already had a history of high inflation under Tito, but after the collapse of eastern European communism in 1989, the country's leaders began to pursue ever more irrational economic policies, printing money to finance deficits and, later, to fund the war effort as the country split. It took five revaluations, and an immense amount of economic pain, before the currency finally stabilised.

The civil aviation industry estimates that 8,000 bags are misrouted on the world's airways every day.

'AVIATION, TERRORISM AND SECURITY'
EDITED BY PAUL WILKINSON AND BRIAN M JENKINS

21 per cent of Americans say they are regularly 'bored out of their mind', and 3.8 per cent have sought counselling for boredom.

'ATLAS OF EXPERIENCE' BY LOUISE VAN SWAAIJ AND JEAN KLARE

60 per cent of newborn babies in India would be in intensive care if born in California.

STATE OF THE WORLD 2000

Every day, five US soldiers try to kill themselves. Before the Iraq war, there was less than one suicide attempt a day.

CNN.COM, 3RD FEBRUARY 2008

An asteroid large enough to wipe out France came within 800,000 km of hitting Earth in August 2001 – it was spotted only days before it hurtled past.

TIME, 21ST JANUARY 2002

In England, Scotland and Wales, about 10 per cent of 5–15 year olds suffer from a mental disorder.

OFFICE FOR NATIONAL STATISTICS

By 2009, each British person working in the private sector will be paying more each month into the pension of a civil servant than into their own pension.

CENTRERIGHT.COM, 15TH JANUARY 2008

80 per cent of cancer cases are caused by environmental factors.

'LIVING DOWNSTREAM' BY SANDRA STEINGRABER

One in 60 men born in Britain in 1953 had a conviction for a
sex offence by the time he was 40.
'TAKING STOCK: WHAT DO WE KNOW ABOUT VIOLENCE?' ESRC

Britain's skilled-worker brain drain problem is the worst in the
world. As of late 2005, over 1.44m graduates had left
Britain, outweighing the 1.26m immigrant graduates,
leaving a net loss of 200,000.
THE INDEPENDENT, 25TH OCTOBER 2005

38 per cent of Jewish Israelis say they think Israel should be
run by religious law, and 30 per cent say Yigal Amir,
murderer of Yitzhak Rabin, should be pardoned.
NEW YORKER, 30TH JULY 2007

Drinking alcohol is a factor in more than half of violent crimes
and a third of domestic violence.
BRITISH MEDICAL JOURNAL, DECEMBER 2007

Smoking is responsible for 25 per cent of all male deaths in the
developed world.
WORLD HEALTH ORGANISATION

Almost two thirds of Palestinians think violence has achieved
more than negotiations.
PALESTINIAN CENTRE FOR POLICY AND SURVEY RESEARCH

After the end of donor anonymity, as of May 2007 there were
only 205 sperm donors registered in Britain.
BBC NEWS ONLINE, 16TH MAY 2007

70 per cent of the trade tariffs paid by developing countries are
to other developing countries.
FORMER US WTO AMBASSADOR LINNET DEILY

In Britain, 86 per cent of rough sleepers are drug addicts.

CRACKDOWN, SOHO ANTI-DRUGS CAMPAIGN

There are 87.4 violent deaths per 100,000 population in
Lithuania: the highest figure in the world.

WORLD HEALTH ORGANISATION

96 per cent of Jamaicans with an advanced education emigrate.

FOREIGN POLICY, SEPTEMBER/OCTOBER 2004

When an unprotected PC running Windows goes online,
there is a 50 per cent chance it will be 'compromised' –
pick up a virus, spyware or some another malicious
infection – within 12 minutes.

SOPHOS

In the US in 2002, only six undergraduates earned Arabic
language degrees.

SLATE, 4TH OCTOBER 2004

A boy born in Russia in 2004 had a lower life expectancy than
one born in Bangladesh.

NEW YORKER, 11TH OCTOBER 2004

A 2004 poll of British workers found that fewer than 5 per cent
could count up to 20 in a foreign language.

BBC NEWS ONLINE, 30TH JULY 2004

Nearly 35,000 nurses – enough to staff the entire health service
in Wales – emigrated from Britain between 2003 and
2007.

THE TIMES, 28TH JANUARY 2008

The life expectancy of professional cyclists is about 50.

NEW CRITERION, JUNE 2004

A third of the world's obese people live in developing countries.

'50 FACTS THAT SHOULD CHANGE THE WORLD'
BY JESSICA WILLIAMS

In the London borough of Lambeth, there are more than 100
pregnancies for every 1,000 females aged 15–17.

OFFICE FOR NATIONAL STATISTICS

The Scottish suicide rate is almost double that of England: 21
per 100,000 people compared with 12 per 100,000.

FINANCIAL TIMES, 16TH JANUARY 2004

There are more than 1,000 chemicals in coffee. 27 of these
were tested on rodents; 19 were carcinogenic.

BBC RADIO 4

Anyone who has spent much of the last decade in Britain cannot have failed to notice the vertiginous growth in CCTV cameras. Yet it still comes as a shock to discover that, according to a report in the *Daily Telegraph* in May 2007, the ***5m CCTV cameras in Britain make up one fifth of the world's total.*** Yet while concerns over privacy do seem to be on the rise – and one study found that lampposts were seven times as effective at cutting crime than CCTV cameras – it seems that CCTV is genuinely popular: polls suggest about 75 per cent of us want more, not less, surveillance.

Britons drink a quarter more alcohol than they did ten years ago.
THE ECONOMIST, 3RD SEPTEMBER 2005

In the US, 12 per cent of Coca-Cola is consumed with or for breakfast.
'THE GREAT AMERICA FOOD ALMANAC' BY IRENA CHALMERS

About 90 per cent of the planet's disease burden falls on poor countries. Just 3 per cent of drug company R&D is aimed at such diseases.
THE ECONOMIST, 16TH APRIL 2005

In São Paulo, 10 per cent of all homicides are committed by police officers.
VEJA

The percentage of new recruits to the US army with high-school diplomas fell from 94 per cent in 2003 to 71 per cent in 2007.
SLATE, 24TH JANUARY 2008

By 2050, Britain will be paying out £6.5bn in benefits and
£1.3bn in healthcare costs to British pensioners living
overseas.

PUBLIC POLICY RESEARCH, MARCH/MAY 2007

Over half the organs used in transplant surgery in China come
from judicial executions.

HUMAN RIGHTS WATCH WORLD REPORT 2007

Under Gorbachev, 5 per cent of senior Soviet officials had a
background in the armed forces or security services.
Under Putin, the figure was 78 per cent.

HARPER'S, MAY 2007

Bird flu kills someone almost every week in Indonesia.

AP, 24TH APRIL 2007

Venezuela has the highest per capita murder rate in the world.

FOREIGN POLICY, MAY/JUNE 2007

In July 2007, 141 people in China were killed by lightning
strikes.

BBC NEWS ONLINE, 2ND AUGUST 2007

Ukraine's population is expected to fall by 43 per cent from its
2004 level by 2050.

THE ECONOMIST, 7TH JANUARY 2005

Between 20 and 50 per cent of deaths from hypothermia involve
paradoxical undressing (the sufferer removing their own
clothes).

NEW SCIENTIST, 21ST APRIL 2007

By the age of 50, the human eye lets in 20 per cent less light.

LOS ANGELES TIMES, 17TH FEBRUARY 2004

In the US, the lifetime parental cost of rearing one middle-class child is about $1.43m.

'FAMILY BUSINESS' EDITED BY HELEN WILKINSON

In Britain, about 30 per cent of graduate women born in the early 1960s entered their forties childless. For graduate women born in 1970, the expected figure is 40 per cent.

PROSPECT, APRIL 2006

Suicide is the biggest killer among young Chinese. It accounts for a third of all deaths among rural women.

MARGINAL REVOLUTION, 30TH JUNE 2006

In the US, on the third and fourth days after heavyweight championship bouts, the homicide rate rises by an average 9 per cent.

'HAPPINESS' BY RICHARD LAYARD

At any given moment, there are about 1,800 thunderstorms happening around the world. Approximately 100 lightning bolts strike the earth every second.

WEATHERMETRICS.COM

In Kansas and Massachusetts, the minimum age for marriage is 12.

CHICAGO TRIBUNE, 11TH DECEMBER 2004

In 2003, Japan accepted 26 asylum-seekers out of 2,694 applications.

NEW STATESMAN, 21ST FEBRUARY 2005

In the US, half of all children aged 4–6 have played video games, and a quarter say they do so regularly.

BOSTON GLOBE MAGAZINE, 20TH FEBRUARY 2005

There are more African scientists and engineers working in the US than in the whole of Africa.

COMMISSION FOR AFRICA REPORT, 2005

In the US, 36 per cent of newly-wed couples have already had a physically violent argument.

EDGE.ORG

Mein Kampf was the second bestselling book in Turkey in March 2005.

HARPER'S, JUNE 2005

Two per cent of the electricity used by a lightbulb is converted into light, the rest into heat.

'COUNTDOWN TO A FAIRER WORLD', NEW INTERNATIONALIST

Britons buy almost half as many celebrity magazines as Americans, despite a population only a fifth the size.

THE ECONOMIST, 3RD SEPTEMBER 2005

In 2005, there were over 25,000 centenarians in Japan – twice as many as there were five years earlier. By 2050, the country expects to have over 1m people aged over 100.

ASSOCIATED PRESS, 13TH SEPTEMBER 2005

Of the 218 new plays produced in Britain in 2004, only 38 were written by women.

THE GUARDIAN, 10TH SEPTEMBER 2005

Half of all Australians will contract skin cancer at some point in their lives.

SUNDAY TIMES, 11TH APRIL 2004

There are as many fake doctors practising in India as real ones.

HARPER'S, MAY 2008

In New Zealand, because of male emigration, a 32-year-old
woman has as much chance of finding a partner her
age as does an 82-year-old woman.

POPULATION GROWTH REPORT 2005

Only 26 per cent of Pakistanis and Bangladeshis in Britain are
fluent in English. The equivalent figure for the US is 68
per cent.

DAVID CAMERON SPEECH, FOREIGN POLICY CENTRE

In some developed countries, people born after 1953 are three
times more likely to suffer from depression than their
grandparents.

'THE LOSS OF HAPPINESS IN MARKET DEMOCRACY' BY ROBERT LANE

In 1996 in China, there were 121 boys between the ages of one
and four for every 100 girls in the same age range.

CHRONICLE OF HIGHER EDUCATION, 30TH APRIL 2004

The most widely known fact about George Bush Snr in the 1992
presidential election was that he hated broccoli.
86 per cent of likely voters knew that the Bushes' dog
was called Millie; only 15 per cent knew that Bush
and Clinton both favoured the death penalty.

NEW YORKER, 30TH AUGUST 2004

In 2007, YouTube consumed as much bandwidth as the entire
internet did in 2000.

NEW YORK TIMES, 13TH MARCH 2008

European countries are expected to put about 50 coal-fired
plants into operation over the next five years.

NEW YORK TIMES, 23RD APRIL 2008

There are half a million semi-automatic machine guns in Swiss homes.

'50 FACTS YOU NEED TO KNOW: EUROPE' BY EMMA HARTLEY

There were 658 suicide bombings around the world in 2007 – more than double the number in any of the last 25 years. Afghanistan and Iraq were responsible for 542 of these.

WASHINGTON POST, 18TH APRIL 2008

Every year 1.2m people die in road accidents around the world.

THE OBSERVER, 23RD MARCH 2008

HOW THE WORLD WORKS

Facts about the unexpected operations
of the world and the people in it

90 per cent of British trade is conducted by sea.

THE GUARDIAN, 23RD OCTOBER 2004

An estimated 30 per cent of the earth's ice-free land is directly or indirectly involved in livestock production.

NEW YORK TIMES, 27TH JANUARY 2008

24 per cent of the world's construction cranes are operating in Dubai.

GULF NEWS, 18TH JUNE 2006

An extra ten mobile phones per 100 people in a typical developing country leads to an additional 0.59 percentage points of growth in GDP per person.

THE ECONOMIST, 10TH MAY 2007

Each year, 30,000–80,000 meteorites land on earth.

NATURAL HISTORY MUSEUM

Homosexual behaviour occurs in more than 450 different kinds of animals.

'BIOLOGICAL EXUBERANCE' BY BRUCE BAGEMIHL

Nature reserves and national parks cover 3 per cent of the world's surface.

PANOS MEDIA BRIEFING NO 25

The removal of the annual half-ton of droppings from Nelson's column in Trafalgar Square costs London about £35,000 per year.

'MERDE' BY RALPH A LEWIN

In Britain, of the 200,000 books on sale in 2007, only 10,000 sold over 3,500 copies.

THE TIMES, 16TH FEBRUARY 2008

With its foreign exchange reserves, China could buy every
single publicly quoted African company.

ECONOMIST.COM, 29TH JULY 2007

The richest 1 per cent of households in Britain pay 21 per cent of
income tax and the top 10 per cent pay 50 per cent.

INSTITUTE FOR FISCAL STUDIES

90 per cent of American firms are family-owned, and around
a third of Fortune 500 companies are at least partly
family-managed. Family businesses account for two
thirds of employment in the EU.

'DYNASTIES: FORTUNES AND MISFORTUNES OF THE WORLD'S GREAT
FAMILY BUSINESSES' BY DAVID S LANDES

Exports make up a higher proportion of GDP in Britain than
in France, Germany, Japan or the US.

LIAM BYRNE SPEECH

In 2007, China replaced the US as Japan's largest trading
partner.

PEOPLE'S DAILY ONLINE, 27 APRIL 2007

Britain has 47,800 PR people to 45,000 journalists.

'FLAT EARTH NEWS' BY NICK DAVIES

Nearly half of the carbon dioxide emitted by humans since the
beginning of the 19th century has been absorbed by the
oceans.

NEW YORKER, 20TH NOVEMBER 2006

A penny dropped from the top of the Empire State Building
would do no more than sting a pedestrian at ground
level.

LIVESCIENCE.COM

The rapid growth of China is a major factor behind the high global prices of natural resources and construction materials – that much is old news. But Chinese hunger is literal as well as metaphorical – as the country grows and people become richer, an increasing number are turning to western diets. And the impact is felt globally: in September 2007, the *New York Times* reported that **global milk prices doubled from 2005 to 2007**, driven in part by a tripling in annual per capita milk consumption in China from two gallons in 2000 to six gallons in 2007. The country is now the leading importer of milk in the world, and if it continues to maintain annual double-digit growth rates, the world may just have to get used to high prices for agricultural staples.

99 per cent of European gross national income stays within member states and just 1 per cent goes to Brussels.

DENIS MACSHANE

Indonesia has higher net carbon emissions per year than the US when forest clearances and fires are taken into account.

PROSPECT, APRIL 2007

Air weighs roughly one kilogram per cubic metre. Large rooms contain several tonnes of air.

'AN OCEAN OF AIR: A NATURAL HISTORY OF THE ATMOSPHERE' BY GABRIELLE WALKER

Spammers usually need to send one million emails to get 15 positive responses.

NEW YORKER, 6TH AUGUST 2007

Europe's merchant ships emit around a third more carbon than aircraft do.

THE ECONOMIST, 10TH JUNE 2006

A tenth of the world's population relies on the river Ganges for water.

BBC WORLD

In 2007, sales of physical music (mainly CDs) fell 19 per cent in the US.

THE ECONOMIST, 10TH JANUARY 2008

Half the world's supertankers are disassembled at Chittagong port in Bangladesh.

FOREIGN POLICY, JANUARY/FEBRUARY 2006

More than 30 per cent of the technology firms created in Silicon Valley since the 1980s have been founded by entrepreneurs with Indian or Chinese roots.

THE ECONOMIST, 6TH MAY 2006

Men and women differ genetically by 1 to 2 per cent – as wide a gap as the one that separates women from female chimpanzees.

BOSTON GLOBE, 6TH JULY 2003

In Britain, 1.3 per cent of the population live in towns or villages of fewer than 2,000 people.

OFFICE OF NATIONAL STATISTICS

Each year Ireland generates 869kg of waste per head, 25 per cent more than Denmark, its nearest EU rival. Britain's figure is 600kg.

THE ECONOMIST, 2ND SEPTEMBER 2006

Although more than 70 per cent of British imports enter the country by water, less than 1 per cent of British freight is carried on the inland waterway system, compared to over 20 per cent in Germany.

SUNDAY TIMES, 8TH OCTOBER 2006

Given the right conditions, over seven years a pair of poppies will produce 820,000 million million million descendants.
NEW SCIENTIST, 27TH NOVEMBER 2004

In Britain, 1–2 per cent of births are through IVF.
THE TIMES, 14TH MARCH 2005

Our eyes are always the same size from birth, but our nose and ears never stop growing.
BBC ONLINE

In 1983, Los Angeles had three times as many workers in the aerospace industry as in the movie industry. By 2000, the proportions were reversed.
PROSPECT, MARCH 2004

A third of all British legislation and 70 per cent of our economic and social legislation originates from Brussels.
'THE BRITISH SPRING', DEMOS

8 to 15 per cent of the increase in American life expectancy over the last 30 years comes from people moving to warmer climates.
NEW YORK TIMES, 12TH JANUARY 2008

In 2005 the 54 billionaires in Britain paid a total of £14.7m in income tax. Of this, £9m was contributed by James Dyson.
SUNDAY TIMES, 3RD DECEMBER 2006

Switzerland imports 24 per cent of the world's caviar.
WORLD WILDLIFE FUND

On an average evening, between 30 and 45 paparazzi follow Britney Spears around.
THE ATLANTIC, APRIL 2008

In 2004, 90 per cent of the world's pianos were made in China, South Korea and Japan.

THE INDEPENDENT, 30TH OCTOBER 2004

Despite not being a member of the EU, Norway pays around half the British budgetary contribution for the right to participate in the single market.

PROSPECT RESEARCH

Serbia produces almost a third of the world's raspberries.

US DEPARTMENT OF AGRICULTURE

The Arts Council typically spends around 90 per cent of its annual music budget on opera.

PROSPECT RESEARCH

Half of animal species are parasites.

NATURE, 6TH JULY 2000

In the US, more than 1m elections are held over every four-year period.

'BRING HOME THE REVOLUTION' BY JONATHAN FREEDLAND

Mexican migrants in the US send home almost $23bn a month in remittances. In the first half of 2006, remittances grew 23 per cent compared with the same period the previous year, but in the first half of 2007 they grew just 0.6 per cent year-on-year.

FINANCIAL TIMES, 12TH DECEMBER 2007

More than 90 per cent of the world's rubies come from Burma.

SUNDAY TIMES, 30TH SEPTEMBER 2007

The combined budget for quangos in Britain is five times that of the ministry of defence.

THE SUN, 20TH AUGUST 2007

Vietnam is the second largest producer of coffee in the world, after Brazil. It produces 20 times as much as Uganda.

PROSPECT RESEARCH

When rainfall is significantly below normal, the risk of low-level conflict escalating to full-scale civil war approximately doubles in the following year.

NEW SCIENTIST, 2ND JUNE 2007

658,644 new houses were built in Spain in 2006, while 168,000 were built in England. This means Spain built five times more houses per head.

STEPHEN NICKELL, NUFFIELD COLLEGE

Cash was used for 60 per cent of retail transactions in Britain in 2007 – up from 54 per cent in 2006 – and accounted for a third of all money spent.

BRITISH RETAIL CONSORTIUM

Gone
TO THE D🐕GS

Facts about the rubbishness of modern life

About 25 per cent of American workers in the private sector get
no paid holiday at all.

NEW REPUBLIC, 30TH JULY 2007

In Britain, 93 per cent of young people can master a computer
game while only 38 per cent can bake a potato.

CENTRE FOR FOOD POLICY

Of the 10,500 athletes who competed in the 2004 Olympics,
only 11 were openly gay.

OUTSPORTS.COM

Only one in every 400 stop and searches carried out under
the British anti-terrorism laws leads to an arrest. In
2005–06, one force, City of London, carried out 6,846
stops of pedestrians and vehicles without finding
enough evidence to justify a single arrest.

THE GUARDIAN, 31ST OCTOBER 2007

70 per cent of Israel's kibbutzim are now at least partially
privatised.

HARPER'S, NOVEMBER 2007

Since 1979, the share of pre-tax income going to the top 1 per
cent of American households has risen by 7 percentage
points, to 16 per cent. Over the same span, the share of
income going to the bottom 80 per cent has fallen by
7 percentage points.

NEW YORK TIMES MAGAZINE, 10TH JUNE 2007

The Ronald Reagan Presidential Library has lost more than
80,000 of its artefacts (gifts to the president) out of its
collection of 100,000.

LOS ANGELES TIMES, 8TH NOVEMBER 2007

British governments of every shade are continually dogged by claims that the unemployment figures they publish fail to represent the true extent of joblessness in the country. One of the accusations is that buried within the vast numbers of people on incapacity benefits – around 2.65m at the time of writing – are a significant number who are capable of work. *Many people cite the proportion of those on incapacity benefit who claim mental health problems – in late 2005 the* Guardian *reported this figure to be 38 per cent.* Some think this shows that we have become far too eager to 'pathologise' normal reactions to difficult circumstances; others believe that depression is indeed a major problem and that a large-scale programme of government investment in therapists would eventually pay for itself by getting hundreds of thousands off incapacity benefit.

The average British commute is one hour and five minutes. In 2003 it was 35 minutes.

THE GUARDIAN, 21ST JANUARY 2008

Total annual health expenditure for the 900m people in Africa is £9.8bn – less than a tenth of the cost of the NHS, catering for 60m.

PROSPECT RESEARCH

On average, British Airways loses nine sets of luggage for every jumbo flight.

THE GUARDIAN, 23RD FEBRUARY 2008

20 per cent of a police officer's average working day is spent on filling out forms.

DAILY MAIL, 21ST FEBRUARY 2008

In 2006, for the first time, more French children were born out of wedlock than to married parents.

REUTERS, 15TH JANUARY 2008

In Britain, five times as much money is taken from motorists in taxes as is spent on transport. In the US the figures are equal.

BBC ONLINE

A survey in 2007 found that more than 70 per cent of Germans, Italians, Spaniards and Britons, and 64 per cent of Americans, had not had a person from an ethnic minority to their home for dinner over the previous year. In France, 56 per cent had not.

INTERNATIONAL HERALD TRIBUNE, 24TH MAY 2007

Only five countries have never had a single female member of government: Lebanon, Monaco, Saudi Arabia, Tonga and the Vatican.

WORLDWIDE GUIDE TO WOMEN IN LEADERSHIP

As of late 2006, the British rail system was receiving almost £5bn a year in public subsidy – almost four times as much as it did when privatised in 1994.

THE ECONOMIST, 2ND DECEMBER 2006

Only half of American adults have read a book since leaving high school.

RANDOM HOUSE

In Britain, between 1991 and 2005, deaths directly attributed to alcohol almost doubled.

BRITISH MEDICAL JOURNAL, DECEMBER 2007

Since 2002, more than $676m worth of art has been stolen from
European museums.

FOREIGN POLICY 'PASSPORT', 11TH FEBRUARY 2008

In the 20th century, democratic government turned into
authoritarian rule more than 70 times.

FOREIGN AFFAIRS, MAY/JUNE 1999

40 per cent of heterosexual British men say they would be
justified in hitting their partner if she was unfaithful,
and 20 per cent if they thought she was neglecting
their children.

'DOES CRIMINAL JUSTICE WORK?', CRIME AND SOCIETY FOUNDATION

47 per cent of under-fives in India are malnourished – more
than in sub-Saharan Africa.

THE ECONOMIST, 6TH JANUARY 2007

Only 0.4 per cent of households in Lagos have a toilet
    connected to a sewage system.

NEW YORKER, 13TH NOVEMBER 2006

In the US, adult bookshops outnumber McDonald's restaurants
    three to one.

'EFFECT OF PORNOGRAPHY ON WOMEN AND CHILDREN'
US SENATE JUDICIARY COMMITTEE

Between 25,000 and 100,000 Indian farmers commit suicide
    every year.

THE HINDU, 25TH FEBRUARY 2007

50 per cent of the entire wealth of Russia is in the hands of just
    500 people.

SKY

47 per cent of British men and 35 per cent of women say they
    would give up sex for six months in exchange for a
    50-inch plasma HD television. But only 17 per cent
    of men would stop watching football.

THE REGISTER, 11TH FEBRUARY 2008

The US reached the 1m lawyer mark in 2000.

TIMES LITERARY SUPPLEMENT, 13TH OCTOBER 2000

An estimated 7,000 Americans a year die as a result of doctors'
    bad handwriting.

HARPER'S, APRIL 2007

Only a quarter of British state school pupils with an A and
    two Bs at A-level are admitted to a top university,
    against 45 per cent of independent school pupils
    with the same qualifications.

THE GUARDIAN, 27TH MARCH 2007

In 2006, the average Russian drank 26 pints of alcohol – three times as much as in 1990, and more than half as much again as in 2005. Alcohol was responsible for 28,386 deaths – 12 per cent of the Russian total – but this represented a fall from 2005's number of 40,877.

PHYSORG.COM

Properties in London costing more than £2m outnumber those costing less than £100,000.

THE LONDON PAPER, 9TH MAY 2007

In 2006, more than 70,000 pupils who should have been taking a GCSE did not turn up to the exam.

THE OBSERVER, 6TH MAY 2007

41 per cent of British full-time employees work over 40 hours a week, compared to 16 per cent in France and 9 per cent in Sweden.

EUROSTAT

In 2006, the Swedish town of Södertälje took in twice as many Iraqi refugees as the entire US.

NEW YORK TIMES, 13TH JUNE 2007

In a 2002 survey, 52 per cent of Russians said they thought America 'got what it deserved' on 9/11.

THE TIMES, 12TH SEPTEMBER 2002

When Tony Blair came to power there were 129 shoplifters in prison; when he left there were 1,400. In 1997 there were fewer than 4,000 life prisoners; in 2007, there were 6,431 – more than Germany, France, Italy and Turkey combined.

THE GUARDIAN, 20TH JUNE 2007

Around 25 Palestinian activists have adopted the name Hitler or Abu Hitler.

IRIS

About half of British households do not have a dining table.

THE TIMES, 22ND OCTOBER 2004

It's a noticeable feature of the race to become US president in 2008 that the two candidates – Republican John McCain and Democrat Barack Obama – are both figures with significant cross-party and independent appeal. McCain, while at pains during the Republican primaries to bolster his credentials as a 'conservative', has throughout his political career staked out a number of positions that have hardly endeared him to the American right. He was an early proponent of the need to take action on climate change, and he has been outspoken in his opposition to some of the more extreme interrogation techniques used by the US military and the CIA. Obama, meanwhile, has rested his entire campaign on the idea that America needs to heal its bitter partisan splits if it is to face up to the challenges of the 21st century. Perhaps one of the reasons Obama's message has proved so appealing is that America has grown sick of the rancour that has increasingly characterised its politics over recent years, something well illustrated by the fact, as reported in *USA Today* in the run-up to the 2004 presidential election, that *both John Kerry and George W Bush were rated as 'highly unfavourable' by more voters than any major-party presidential candidate since Barry Goldwater in 1964.* Let's hope the 2008 campaign can draw the cynicism out of ordinary Americans' attitude to politics.

The number of Americans who say they consider themselves to be among the 'have-nots' has risen from 17 to 34 per cent since 1988.

HARPER'S, JANUARY 2008

Of all Oxbridge graduates working as teachers, 54 per cent are teaching in private schools.

SUTTON TRUST

Every eight minutes, someone is deported from Britain.

HOME OFFICE

Britain is responsible for half the potato crisp consumption of Europe.

BBC RADIO 4, 15TH MAY 2006

In 1985, a third of under-25s in Britain owned their own home. Now the figure is under a quarter.

THE OBSERVER, 21ST MAY 2006

In 2001, nearly one in five GP patients had at least one allergic disease. But by 2005, that figure had increased to nearly one in four.

DAILY MAIL, 16TH JULY 2007

81 per cent of British Muslims consider themselves Muslim first and British second. This is a higher proportion than in Jordan, Egypt or Turkey, and exceeded only by Pakistan.

THE GUARDIAN, 11TH AUGUST 2006

One in three school-aged girls in Turkey does not attend school; in the Kurdish region, only 14 per cent of girls attend secondary school.

THE ECONOMIST, 29TH JULY 2006

There is only one ATM in Afghanistan.

FOREIGN OFFICE

In Britain, football sendings-off have increased by 3,658 per cent since the first half of the 20th century.

TIMES LITERARY SUPPLEMENT, 8TH APRIL 2005

Britain and Iceland are the only two developed countries in which schoolchildren can drop history at the age of 14.

BBC NEWS ONLINE, 27TH JANUARY 2005

In the US, half of men say they feel nervous in the company of women.

'CONVERSATION' BY THEODORE ZELDIN

Just 3.5 per cent of British people believe they are in the top income quartile; 47 per cent believe they are in the bottom.

PROSPECT, JANUARY 2005

The percentage of Nigerians living on less than a dollar a day has risen from 32 per cent in 1985 to 71 per cent today.

HARPER'S, FEBRUARY 2007

One in five children cannot name an activity they have done with their fathers in the past week. One third of all children never see their absent parent following family breakdown.

NSPCC

The Mafia accounts for 7 per cent of Italian GDP, more than any single business.

LOS ANGELES TIMES, 13TH APRIL 2008

A quarter of British students drop out of university.

THE GUARDIAN, 23RD FEBRUARY 2008

In 2001 there was not a single traffic light in the Palestinian
territories.

NEW YORK REVIEW OF BOOKS, 22ND JUNE 2006

70 per cent of mental health in-patients are smokers, compared
to 26 per cent of the general population.

MENTAL HEALTH TODAY

The US earned more tariff revenues in 2001 from Bangladeshi
goods ($331m) than from French ($330m). Bangladeshi
exports were worth $2bn and French $30bn.

PROGRESSIVE POLICY INSTITUTE

Two thirds of British pensioners say they would be happy to
receive medical treatment abroad, more than in any
other major European country.

POPULUS

Across the OECD, green taxes made up an average of 5.6 per
cent of the total tax take in 2005 – down from 5.9 per
cent in 1996.

ECONOMIST.COM, 31ST MARCH 2008

The price of lead has risen sevenfold in the last six years. Some
English churches have had their roofs stripped of lead
by thieves hoping to sell it on.

NEW YORK TIMES, 8TH APRIL 2008

The Czech Republic and Poland are the only two EU countries
whose domestic films earn more overseas than the
government provides in subsidy to the film industry.

MARGINAL REVOLUTION, 29TH MAY 2007

FUNNY
Foreigners

Facts about the peculiar habits
of other countries

20 per cent of all luxury goods are sold in Japan and another
30 per cent to Japanese travelling abroad – meaning
Japanese buy half of all luxury goods in the world.

'DELUXE: HOW LUXURY LOST ITS LUSTRE' BY DANA THOMAS

In 1990, it was made illegal in Iran for Iranian women to marry
Afghan men.

PROSPECT RESEARCH

China drinks far more beer than any other nation. However,
Snow, China's most popular beer, commands only
about 5 per cent of the domestic market.

ECONOMIST.COM, 16TH OCTOBER 2007

In Denmark, people buying a new car must pay a registration
fee of approximately 105 per cent of the car's value.

WALL STREET JOURNAL, 16TH APRIL 2007

Only 31 per cent of Christian activists in the US believe that a
person can be both a good Christian and a liberal.

INSTITUTE FOR FIRST AMENDMENT STUDIES

France has 36,782 mayors – more than two fifths of the 88,000
across the EU. There are elected mayors of five villages
which ceased to exist 92 years ago.

THE INDEPENDENT, 29TH FEBRUARY 2008

The average person in Luxembourg drinks 15.5 litres of alcohol
a year – more than any other country. The British drink
just under 12.

WORLD HEALTH ORGANISATION

In Milan, it is a legal requirement to smile at all times, except
during funerals or hospital visits.

LAW SOCIETY

In Japan, only the most major streets have names.

PLANET TOKYO

The Indian government will give $250 in cash, plus a certificate of appreciation, to anyone who marries a Dalit, or 'untouchable'. In Madhya Pradesh, a state of 60m people, only 97 couples in the last fiscal year claimed the award.

LOS ANGELES TIMES, 4TH NOVEMBER 2007

There are no legal public cinemas in Saudi Arabia.

INTERNATIONAL HERALD TRIBUNE, 29TH APRIL 2006

You will not be surprised to hear that Iran is not a good place to be gay. Male and female homosexuality is punishable by lashes or even death in the Islamic Republic, and the regime has not shied away from applying corporal or capital punishment to those who flout the law, including teenage boys. (Despite this, the country's president is on record as saying there are no homosexuals in Iran, which leads one to wonder what all those people are being executed for.) Transsexuality, however, is an entirely different proposition. The *Guardian* reported in September 2007 that *according to official figures, Iran has between 15,000 and 20,000 transsexuals* – although some believe the true figure may be as much as ten times higher – and that it performs more sex change operations than any other country bar Thailand. In 1983, Ayatollah Khomeini passed a fatwa authorising such operations, and his successor Khamenei reinforced it. Transsexuality is still considered a sickness – as opposed to a sin – and individuals who have undergone sex changes are prone to abuse and stigmatisation. Still, it's got to beat 100 lashes.

The Japanese national anthem is only five lines long. The words were taken from a 10th-century anthology of poetry. The translation is: 'May the reign of the emperor / continue for a thousand, nay, eight thousand generations / and for the eternity that it takes / for small pebbles to grow into a great rock / and become covered with moss.'

ABOUT.COM

Only 15 per cent of Estonians believe in God, making them the least religious nation in the EU.

METRO, 6TH JUNE 2007

Until 1977, German men had the legal right to forbid their wives to take paid employment.

'THE END OF MASCULINITY' BY JOHN MACINNES

About 25 per cent of the Norwegian workforce is absent from work on any given day.

'DISCOVER YOUR INNER ECONOMIST' BY TYLER COWEN

40 per cent of Americans polled in May 2006 said they had no plans to take a summer holiday.

CONFERENCE BOARD

Australia spends more on sport than defence, and ten times more per head on sport than Britain.

THE AUSTRALIAN INSTITUTE OF SPORT

In Brazil, 62 per cent of higher education students are women.

BRAZILIAN EDUCATION MINISTRY

80 per cent of Russian citizens describe themselves as middle class, even though a quarter live below the poverty line.

UPI

In 1996, Mahathir Mohamad, prime minister of Malaysia, threw the largest ever dinner party. 12,000 guests celebrated the 50th anniversary of Mahathir's ruling party, the United Malays National Organisation.

BBC WORLD SERVICE

In the US, 75 per cent of money given away by philanthropists goes to higher education.

ANTHONY GIDDENS

In 1983, a Soviet factory made 13,000 pairs of sunglasses so dark that wearers could look directly at the sun and not see it.

TASS NEWS AGENCY

In Paraguay, duelling is legal if both participants are registered blood donors.

THE GUARDIAN WORLD CUP 2006 GUIDE

In the heyday of protectionism in South Korea, people violating foreign-currency regulations were subject to the death penalty.

BOOKFORUM, FEBRUARY/MARCH 2008

In San Francisco in 1999, 25 overweight people picketed a
health club to protest against an advertisement saying
that when space aliens encounter humans, 'they will
eat the fat ones first'.

INTERNATIONAL HERALD TRIBUNE, 17TH FEBRUARY 1999

In the second world war, every Italian soldier in north Africa
carried his own personal espresso machine.

'ESSENTIAL MILITARIA' BY NICHOLAS HOBBES

Hong Kong's fertility rate – 0.98 children per woman – is the
lowest in the world.

CIA FACTBOOK

In 2003, Russians bought more beer than vodka for the first
time ever.

BUSINESS ANALYTICA

57 per cent of marriages in Sudan, 50 per cent in Pakistan and
36 per cent in Saudi Arabia are between first cousins.

'AFTER THE EMPIRE' BY EMMANUEL TODD

Just 1.4 per cent of Iran's population attend Friday prayers.

OPENDEMOCRACY, 14TH FEBRUARY 2006

In India, unlike most advanced democracies, electoral
participation is positively correlated with poverty.

'MAXIMUM CITY' BY SUKETU MEHTA

The Life of Brian was marketed in Sweden with the slogan,
'The film that is so funny, it was banned in Norway.'

INTERNET MOVIE DATABASE

Brazil has more people of African descent than any country
outside Africa.

BBC

Of India's 1.1bn population, only 35m pay income tax.

NEW YORK TIMES, 17TH JANUARY 2007

Every year, an average of 12 Japanese tourists in Paris have to be repatriated due to severe culture shock.

FOREIGN POLICY 'PASSPORT', 23RD DECEMBER 2006

71 per cent of Russians do not see themselves as European.

MOSCOW TIMES, 1ST MARCH 2007

In Italy, until recently, it was not possible to get a haircut on Monday.

FINANCIAL TIMES, 28TH MARCH 2007

About 30 per cent of the Danish workforce changes jobs every year.

WALL STREET JOURNAL, 25TH APRIL 2007

In 1954 Bob Hawke, future Australian prime minister, earned a place in the *Guinness Book of Records* by drinking two and a half pints – a 'yard' – of beer in 11 seconds.

'EVERYTHING YOU DIDN'T NEED TO KNOW ABOUT AUSTRALIA'
BY ADAM WARD

Five of the ten bestselling novels in Japan in 2007 were written on mobile phones.

THE ECONOMIST, 10TH APRIL 2008

20 per cent more babies were born in Berlin in March 2007 – nine months after the World Cup – than in March 2006.

FINANCIAL TIMES, 9TH JUNE 2007

All eight members of the Qatari weightlifting team at the 2000 Olympics were originally Bulgarian.

THE GUARDIAN, 27TH SEPTEMBER 2000

650,000 people in South Korea have a Manchester United credit
card.

INTERNATIONAL HERALD TRIBUNE, 15TH APRIL 2007

India has just 1 per cent of the world's vehicles, but about 10
per cent of annual road fatalities.

FINANCIAL TIMES, 10TH APRIL 2007

14 per cent of US teenagers who call themselves 'evangelical'
or 'born again' have had three or more sexual partners
by age 17, compared to 9 per cent of those who call
themselves mainstream Protestants.

'FORBIDDEN FRUIT: SEX & RELIGION IN THE LIVES OF AMERICAN TEENAGERS'
BY MARK REGNERUS

52 per cent of Korean infants between the ages of three and five
use the internet. They spend an average four hours a
week online.

KOREAN HERALD, 3RD AUGUST 2007

The Purpose-Driven Life, a Christian advice book published
in 2002, is the bestselling hardback in US history.
Over 25m copies have been sold.

THE ECONOMIST, 3RD DECEMBER 2005

In Sweden, prison sentences of over five years are given out only
for serious crimes like drug dealing, murder and rape.
In 2004, only 329 people were serving sentences of over
five years.

NEW YORK TIMES MAGAZINE, 5TH FEBRUARY 2006

Ethiopia's calendar is more than seven years behind that of the
rest of the world. The country held its millennium
celebrations in September 2007.

BBC NEWS

One of the less predictable consequences of Iran's 1979 revolution has been the rise of the self-help book. While book sales in general have fallen in recent years, the self-help genre is flourishing, according to a *New York Times* article by Azadeh Moaveni from May 2007. Self-help books like *Please Do Not Be a Sheep*, whose chapters include 'Grief Therapy' and 'How to Choose Friends', are flying off the shelves, and to these home-grown success stories you can add the fact that *John Gray's* **Men are from Mars, Women are from Venus** *has been a sensation in Iran – in the first two years after its translation into Farsi, the book sold over 50,000 copies, going through eight reprints.* According to Moaveni, the success of the self-help genre in Iran may be a response to the erosion of traditional gender roles as well as the rise of pre-marital sex. *Psychology Today* quotes an expert from Georgetown University who attributes the success of *Men are from Mars...* to the fact that the book emphasises the difference between the sexes in a way that reflects the experiences of men and women in contemporary Iran. Either way, it's not bad for a cultural import from the Great Satan.

In recent years, Japan, Argentina and Brazil have legalised forms of incest.
THE GUARDIAN, 27TH FEBRUARY 2007

Just 6.5 per cent of Chinese government revenue comes from income tax.
WALL STREET JOURNAL, 11TH FEBRUARY 2008

Per capita, more people are diagnosed with skin cancer each week in Scotland than in Australia.
THE GUARDIAN, 24TH FEBRUARY 2006

In 2005 the Texas House of Representatives passed the 'booty bill', prohibiting 'overly sexually suggestive' performances by cheerleaders.

THE ECONOMIST, 2ND SEPTEMBER 2006

The average Japanese has sex 45 times a year, compared with the global average of 103.

JAPAN TIMES, 22ND JUNE 2006

There have been more translations of Kant into Persian over the last decade than into any other language.

NEW REPUBLIC, IST JUNE 2006

The three most corrupt US states, measured by convictions, are Alaska, Mississippi and Louisiana. The least corrupt are Colorado, Wisconsin and Nebraska.

GLOBAL CORRUPTION REPORT 2005

The Da Vinci Code is the bestselling book in French history. A quarter of the population is estimated to have read it.

BUSINESS WEEK, 17TH MAY 2006

New Zealand's child murder rate is 0.9 per 100,000 children, the third worst in the OECD and more than twice the British rate. The overall murder rate is 2.5 per 100,000 people, compared with 1.5 in Britain. And New Zealand has 50 per cent more rapes.

THE TIMES, 7TH AUGUST 2006

In China, on average, people do not exchange their first kiss until the age of 23.

SUNDAY TIMES, 10TH JUNE 2007

Three quarters of young French people say they would like to become civil servants.

THE ECONOMIST, 1ST APRIL 2006

After the death of Princess Diana, Colombia's flower sales rose by 20 per cent.

TORONTO GLOBE AND MAIL, 3RD OCTOBER 1997

One in three Italians finds a job through a relative.

NEW YORK TIMES, 23RD AUGUST 2006

The French consume more tranquillisers per head than any other nation.

GEORGES CALVET

The address of the Australian Broadcasting Corporation in every Australian state capital city is PO Box 9994, after Don Bradman's test batting average of 99.94.

'AUSTRALIA' BY PHILLIP KNIGHTLEY

North Korea declared three days of mourning after Yasser Arafat's death in 2004.

NEW REPUBLIC, 18TH NOVEMBER 2004

About 41 per cent of Chinese schedule sex, as against only 3 per cent of Russians, and 7 per cent of Americans.

BUSINESS WEEK, 10TH MAY 2007

The largest jacuzzi on the west coast of America is owned by Washington State University – it can hold 53 students.

WILSON QUARTERLY, SUMMER 2004

As of early 2005, more houses in China had a DVD player than running hot and cold water.

THE GUARDIAN, 4TH JANUARY 2005

Per capita sales of board games in Germany are higher than anywhere else in the world.

THE ECONOMIST, 19TH FEBRUARY 2005

French males can marry at 18, but females at only 15.

THE GUARDIAN, 30TH MARCH 2005

The Chicago White Sox baseball team starts its midweek games at 7.11pm after a sponsorship deal with 7-Eleven stores.

THE GUARDIAN, 20TH OCTOBER 2006

There are ten applicants for every place on teacher-training courses in Finnish universities.

WASHINGTON POST, 7TH AUGUST 2005

Surnames were illegal in Mongolia from the early 1920s until 1997, when they were legally reintroduced. But 10,000 people still have only one name.

TORONTO GLOBE AND MAIL, 12TH MAY 2004

500 people were trampled to death in Moscow on the day of Stalin's funeral in 1953.

'RUSSIA: A HISTORY' EDITED BY GREGORY FREEZE

The average working week in South Korea is over 45 hours, nearly seven hours longer than any other OECD country.

ECONOMIST.COM, 16TH APRIL 2008

the past

is another country

Facts about the way we used to live

During the first year of the Nazi invasion of the Soviet Union, the Red army issued 800,000 death sentences to its own soldiers.   'NO SIMPLE VICTORY' BY NORMAN DAVIES

From 1964–68, the US government spent over $20bn (in 2007 terms) on the Apollo space programme – 4 per cent of the federal budget.   SUNDAY TIMES MAGAZINE, 7TH OCTOBER 2007

Slavery was legal in Saudi Arabia until the 1960s.   PROSPECT, APRIL 2002

In 1967, 1,353 dependants of veterans of the US civil war were still receiving government benefits.   FOREIGN POLICY 'PASSPORT', 26TH NOVEMBER 2007

The FBI had a 1,427-page dossier on Albert Einstein.   FORWARD, 14TH JUNE 2002

In the 1830s, the population of the island of Ireland was 8m, just 2m less than England, Wales and Scotland combined.   SLUGGER O'TOOLE

Until the late 1960s, men with long hair were not allowed to enter Disneyland.   PROSPECT RESEARCH

The 1461 battle of Towton, in Yorkshire, saw the bloodiest day in British history. At least 20,000 men – 1 per cent of the English male population – were killed.   THE GUARDIAN, 25TH AUGUST 2007

The earliest recorded reference to bagpipes is on a Hittite slab from Asia Minor, which has been dated to 1000 BC.   VISIT SCOTLAND

Spain has been one of Europe's success stories over the past 30 years: after the death in 1975 of General Franco, who had ruled as a dictator for almost 40 years, the country managed to build a robust democracy and turn itself into a flourishing and prosperous modern European state. Yet the Spanish pulled this off only by avoiding uncomfortable questions about their past; something that was starkly illustrated by the finding of Spain's leading newspaper, *El Mundo*, in 2006 that *a third of the country's population believed Franco had been right to overthrow the country's Republican government in 1936*, a move which led to a brutal three-year civil war that drew in Europe's other major powers. Yet there have been signs recently that the 'pact of silence' about the civil war and Franco's subsequent authoritarian rule that most politicians abided by after the general's death is beginning to wane; José Luis Rodríguez Zapatero's Socialist government has passed a 'law of historical memory', which, among other things, grants money to the families of victims on the Republican side of the civil war to exhume their relatives from unmarked graves.

The biggest ever crowd recorded for a women's football game in England was for a match on Boxing Day, 1920, when 53,000 people saw Dick Kerr's Ladies beat St Helen's Ladies 4–0. The FA banned women from playing on league grounds in December 2001.

FA

3,000 guillotine executions were carried out in Paris during the Terror; 10,000 were carried out under the Nazis in 1944 and 1945 alone.

'GUILLOTINE: THE TIMBERS OF JUSTICE' BY ROBERT FREDERICK OPIE

The first year in which there was no recorded lynching of a
    black American was 1952.

BOSTON GLOBE, 2ND DECEMBER 2007

The foreign-born population of the US peaked around 1890,
    at 15 per cent. It is currently around 10 per cent.

ECONOMIST.COM, 23RD MAY 2007

From 1945–55, Britain's bestselling book was EV Rieu's
    translation of the *Odyssey*.

THE GUARDIAN, 24TH JANUARY 2005

On the night before the Queen's coronation in 1953, 30,000
    people slept in the Mall.

MUSEUM OF LONDON

Cambridge University Press only removed the date of creation
    of the world (4004 BC) from its edition of the Bible in
    1900.

'AEONS' BY MARTIN GORST

In 1921, Britain spent more money running Iraq than on its
    health budget.

EMPIRE, CHANNEL 4

From 1946–78, South Korea received nearly as much US aid as
    Africa.

NEW YORKER, 25TH JULY 2005

The 1922 film **Nosferatu** credited 16 people; *The Matrix
    Revolutions* (2003) 701.

THE OBSERVER BOOK OF FILM

Until 1972 in Britain you had to be a householder to sit on
    a jury.

'MIND THE GAP' BY FERDINAND MOUNT

A quarter of the estimated 60,000 witches executed in Europe between 1450 and 1750 were men.

MALE WITCHES IN EARLY MODERN EUROPE

Winston Churchill never visited Australia.

THE OBSERVER, 1ST OCTOBER 2006

In 1715, the British army was roughly the same size as that of the King of Sardinia.

'CAPTIVES' BY LINDA COLLEY

Until the early 1980s, mortgages were rationed in Britain.

BBC NEWS ONLINE, 12TH JUNE 2007

In 1969, an American urologist bought Napoleon's mummified penis at auction.

NEW YORK TIMES, 13TH MAY 2007

In 1910, 20 per cent of the world's Swedes lived in the US.

THE ECONOMIST, 14TH JUNE 2003

Andrew Jackson personally fought in 103 duels.

WASHINGTON MONTHLY, MARCH 2007

History seems to have delivered clear verdicts on the two decisions to go to war in Iraq, in 1991 and then 2003. The first attack on Iraq looks, in retrospect, clearly justified: there was an obvious casus belli – Saddam's invasion and occupation of Kuwait, a sovereign state; there was strong international support, as shown by the fact that the US was able to get the UN security council to pass a resolution authorising war for only the third time in its history; and there was a clear war aim – to remove Iraqi troops from Kuwaiti soil – and exit strategy. The second Iraq war, by contrast, looks like the biggest US foreign policy catastrophe for a generation – it was a war of choice, not necessity, based on intelligence that turned out to be staggeringly inaccurate; it was prosecuted in the teeth of fierce opposition throughout the world; and while there were clear war aims – depose Saddam and disarm Iraq – the lack of pre-war planning for the occupation made, in many people's eyes, the postwar bloodshed and chaos inevitable. Yet a look at the 1991 and 2002 congressional votes on whether to authorise, respectively, President Bush Snr and President Bush Jnr to invade Iraq paints a very different picture. Back in 1991, the vote scraped through the Senate by 52 to 47 votes. As the *Washington Times* reported at the time, had three or more of the ten Democratic senators who voted to authorise war followed the party line and voted against, Bush Snr would have lost the vote. *In 2002, by contrast, the Senate vote was a cakewalk for Bush Jnr, who won the support of 77 of the 100 senators.*

Just after the six-day war, 49 per cent of French people
believed that Israel should annex all of the Palestinian
land it had conquered.
THE OBSERVER, 25TH APRIL 2004

The average woman today has 450 periods over her lifetime,
compared with an estimated 160 in her ancestor's.
PROSPECT, SEPTEMBER 2003

According to the 1851 British census, of the 3.3m people living
in towns and cities, only one third had been born in
the same place.
INTRODUCTION TO CHARLES DICKENS'S 'HARD TIMES' BY DAVID CRAIG

On average, in every year between the middle of the 16th
century and the end of the 17th, Russia expanded
its territory by land area equal to the size of the
Netherlands.
NEW YORK REVIEW OF BOOKS, 7TH OCTOBER 2004

Of the 28 British government departments created between
1960 and 1979, 13 had been wound up by 1981.
COMMENT IS FREE, 29TH MARCH 2007

In the US, the price of a bottle of Coca-Cola remained the
same – 5 cents – from 1886 to 1959.
SLATE, 11TH MAY 2007

A late 1940s survey found that 49 per cent of Britons couldn't
name a single British colony.
'AUSTERITY BRITAIN 1945–51' BY DAVID KYNASTON

In 1900, Americans spent nearly twice as much on funerals as
on medicine, and less than 2 per cent took holidays.
NEW YORK TIMES, 10TH JUNE 2007

When **Woman's Hour** *began* in 1946, it was hosted by a man.

SUNDAY TIMES, 13TH MAY 2007

The last year that Britain exported more goods than she imported was 1846.

PROSPECT RESEARCH

At the beginning of the 18th century, India's GDP was the largest in the world.

TIMES ONLINE, 17TH JANUARY 2003

When Fidel Castro took power in Cuba, he ordered all Monopoly sets to be destroyed.

HASBRO

In 1945, the US was responsible for half of world GDP. The figure is now about 20 per cent.

PAUL KENNEDY LECTURE, LSE, 6TH FEBRUARY 2008

Up to a third of the Libyan population is estimated to have died during the Italian occupation in the 1930s.

NEW YORKER, 8TH MAY 2006

In 1935, 7.5 per cent of Germans were members of the Nazi party, but among teachers the figure was nearly one third.

THE SCOTSMAN, 13TH AUGUST 2007

In 1893, when Arthur Conan Doyle killed off Sherlock Holmes, 20,000 people cancelled their subscriptions to the *Strand* magazine, which had published the Holmes stories.

WILSON QUARTERLY, SUMMER 1999

A third of patent applications in America in 1905 were related to the bicycle.

RSA JOURNAL, WINTER 2005

Catherine de Medici introduced knickers in the 16th century in France, as she preferred to ride side-saddle on horses.

SUNDAY TIMES, 23RD OCTOBER 2005

Soviet-made aeroplanes once made up 26 per cent of the world's aircraft fleet.

WALL STREET JOURNAL, 20TH DECEMBER 2002

Hilaire Belloc served as Liberal MP for Salford.

THE GUARDIAN, 10TH DECEMBER 2007

In 1978, China's economy was smaller than Belgium's.

'THE UNDERCOVER ECONOMIST' BY TIM HARFORD

In central London in the late 17th century, post was delivered ten to 12 times a day.

'AT LARGE AND AT SMALL: CONFESSIONS OF A LITERARY HEDONIST'
BY ANNE FADIMAN

During the 1864–70 Lopez war between Paraguay and the
triple alliance (Argentina, Brazil and Peru), Paraguay's
population fell from 1.3m to 221,000.

'ESSENTIAL MILITARIA' BY NICHOLAS HOBBES

By late 1967, the 5,000 workers at Egypt's El Nasr automotive
plant were producing an average of two vehicles a week.

'SIX DAYS OF WAR' BY MICHAEL OREN

When Hitler invaded the Soviet Union, his army used more
horses, and more horses per soldier, than Napoleon's
invading army had over 100 years earlier.

PROSPECT, APRIL 2002

Ed Balls is the first MP for Normanton not to be a member of
the National Union of Mineworkers.

BBC NEWS ONLINE

Pakistan's first budget devoted nearly two thirds of resources to
defence.

PROSPECT, DECEMBER 2007

In 1928, the British parliament passed the Easter Act, which
fixed Easter Sunday as the first Sunday after the second
Saturday in April. It has never been implemented.

BBC NEWS ONLINE

The calorific value of the typical English diet in 1850 was
roughly equivalent to the average Indian diet today.

'THE ESCAPE FROM HUNGER AND PREMATURE DEATH, 1700–2100'
BY ROBERT FOGEL

In the US, from 1960 to 1974, 128 instrumental pieces of music
reached the top 20, while only 30 did from 1975 to
1990. Since then, there have been just five.

SLATE, 11TH MARCH 2008

double TAKE

Facts that will make your jaw drop

American women are 70 per cent more likely to die in childbirth than Europeans.

TIMES LITERARY SUPPLEMENT, 1ST JUNE 2007

The salary of Ireland's prime minister, or taoiseach, is €310,000 – more than almost any other world leader.

ECONOMIST.COM, 1ST NOVEMBER 2007

Children who bathe every day and wash their hands more than five times a day are 25 per cent more likely to have asthma than those who don't.

JEAN GOLDING, UNIVERSITY OF BRISTOL

37 per cent of blog posts are in Japanese, and 36 per cent in English.

NEW YORK REVIEW OF BOOKS, 14TH FEBRUARY 2008

In 2006, McDonald's sales in France grew by 8 per cent, almost double the growth in America.

NEW YORK SUN, 2ND JULY 2007

In Britain, the mean average weekly wage for foreign-born workers is £424, compared with £395 for the native-born.

THE TIMES, 17TH OCTOBER 2007

In Liverpool, 10 per cent of the members of the Orange Order are black.

'THE FAITHFUL TRIBE' BY RUTH DUDLEY EDWARDS

In the US, the visually impaired and blind watch television for an average 24 hours a week. The most popular programmes are news shows, talk shows and the shopping channels.

AMERICAN FOUNDATION FOR THE BLIND

In two countries – the Ivory Coast and Ghana – the proportion of people who say they have a 'favourable opinion' towards the US is higher than in the US itself.

PEW RESEARCH CENTRE

Ronald Reagan was born six years before John F Kennedy.

PROSPECT RESEARCH

Around 200,000 academic journals are published in the English language. The average number of readers per article is five.

PROSPECT RESEARCH

One ton of computer scrap contains more gold than 17 tons of gold ore.

FOREIGN POLICY, MAY/JUNE 2007

The 2006 World Cup final had a higher US television audience than the 2006 baseball World Series.

NEW REPUBLIC, 17TH JULY 2007

The Finns spend more on ice cream than any other European nation, averaging $110 a head in 2005 – just beating the Italians. Britons spend less than half that figure.

EUROMONITOR

The Harappan civilisation in what is now Pakistan and northwest India had flushing toilets in houses linked with drains in 2500 BC.

SPIKED ONLINE, 30TH OCTOBER 2007

In December 2007, the North Korean women's football team was ranked fifth in the world.

PROSPECT RESEARCH

Women are estimated to buy 80 per cent of everything that
is sold.

'THE WHOLE WOMAN' BY GERMAINE GREER

Worldwide, there are 23,000 different Christian denominations.

'TOWER OF BABEL' BY ROBERT T PENNOCK

The thirty years war in the early 17th century led to the death
of 30 per cent of the population of Germany.

THE ATLANTIC, MARCH 2008

Under Ronald Reagan, federal spending in the US increased by
25 per cent.

SLATE, 9TH FEBRUARY 2001

In Britain, approximately half of all the deaths in people under
40 are caused by head injury.

THE GUARDIAN, 26TH FEBRUARY 2008

In the US, more students learn Latin than Russian, Japanese,
Italian, Mandarin and Cantonese combined.

PROSPECT RESEARCH

William Hague was the first leader of the Conservative party
since 1922 not to become prime minister.

THE GUARDIAN, 8TH JUNE 2001

19 per cent of the Canadian population are immigrants.

FOREIGN POLICY, FEBRUARY 2008

There were 487 homicides in Haiti in 2007; about 5.6 per
100,000 people. The Caribbean's average homicide rate
is 30 per 100,000, making Haiti one of the safest places
in the region.

WASHINGTON TIMES, 8TH MARCH 2008

Anyone who has used the online retailer Amazon will know about the website's user-submitted reviews. For all but the most obscure books, films or CDs, scroll down below the product information and you'll find a number of short assessments written, supposedly, by people just like you, to help you decide whether to buy the item you're looking at. Yet a system that potentially has the power to influence millions of buying decisions was never likely to remain unsullied – and when you consider the incentives introduced by the fact that Amazon ranks its reviewers, you might expect there to be more to the system than the image it presents of straight-up, honest reviews submitted by readers with a bit of time on their hands. And sure enough, when the writer Garth Risk Hallberg did a bit of sniffing around for *Slate* in January 2008, he found out that *Amazon.com's number one reviewer, Harriet Klausner, had averaged 45 reviews a week since 2002.* Polishing off books at this rate has got to rank as pretty near impossible, even for Klausner, who, according to her Amazon profile, is a 'speed reader (a gift I was born with)' who reads 'two books a day'. Hallberg even found out that a user-submitted review of his own book on Amazon by a top ten reviewer had been solicited by his publicist.

Since 1975, there have been nearly 150 terrorist attacks against Americans or American interests in Greece.

FOREIGN POLICY 'PASSPORT', 20TH NOVEMBER 2007

A study of the 101 known suicide bombers in Iraq from March 2003 to February 2006 found that only seven were from Iraq. Eight were from Italy.

NEW REPUBLIC, 22ND JANUARY 2007

High commodity prices and a more assertive foreign policy have once again made Russia a force to contend with. But the country is still struggling against its biggest adversary – death. The death rate in Russia is so much higher than the birth rate that the country is experiencing one of the most drastic declines in population ever known. Estimates vary – the conservative American think tank the Claremont Institute says that Russia is losing 1m people a year, while in 2007 President Putin put the figure at 700,000 – but there is no doubt that the country has got a demographic crisis on its hands. Indeed, *in 2004, the UN's population forecast division predicted that by 2050, there would be more people in Yemen than in Russia.* How the bear has fallen.

A third of the population of Belarus died in the second world war.

THE ECONOMIST, 16TH OCTOBER 2004

One third of all houses in Ireland were built in the last decade.

FINFACTS

30 per cent of published hardback books go directly from the printer to the remainder warehouse.

DAILY TELEGRAPH, 31ST AUGUST 2002

72 per cent of the territory of the countries in the Arab League is in Africa.

MIDDLEEASTNEWS.COM

Middlesbrough is responsible for 25 per cent of national kerb-crawling convictions.

THE WEEK, 28TH JANUARY 2006

The musician Moby (real name Richard Melville Hall), is the great-great-grand-nephew of Herman Melville, author of *Moby Dick*. Moby is a childhood nickname.

SUCCESSWHOSMYDADDY.COM

There are around 7,000 princes in Saudi Arabia's royal clan.

THEGLOBALIST.COM

Lauren Bacall and Shimon Peres are first cousins.

JEWISH BULLETIN, 16TH MAY 2003

Dallas Fort Worth international airport is larger than Manhattan.

'THE GLOBAL SOUL' BY PICO IYER

The oldest Mormon congregation in the world is in Preston.

BBC

German GDP per capita fell below the EU average for the first time in 2004.

THE ECONOMIST, 27TH MARCH 2004

In Britain, flowerpots are responsible for 5,300 accidents a year, making them the second most dangerous piece of garden equipment, after lawnmowers.

THE GUARDIAN, 3RD MAY 2004

Only 5 per cent of land in the US is urbanised.

MICHAEL CRICHTON

Miriam Stoppard is Oona King's aunt.

THE GUARDIAN, 12TH SEPTEMBER 2005

It rains twice as much in Sydney as in London.

THE GUARDIAN, 8TH NOVEMBER 2004

Women make up 70 per cent of Algeria's lawyers and 60 per cent of judges.

NEW YORK TIMES, 26TH MAY 2007

In both Vietnam and the Falklands, more troops committed suicide after the conflict than were killed during it.

PROSPECT RESEARCH

China contributes more than twice as many troops to UN peacekeeping missions as any other member of the security council.

FOREIGN POLICY, 9TH MAY 2006

Rents in central Manchester are 40 per cent higher than in central Manhattan.

CENTRE FOR CITIES

Of the 7.5m people that use television subtitles in Britain, 6m have no hearing impairment.

OFCOM

Nollywood – Nigeria's film industry – produces more films a year than either Hollywood or Bollywood, and is the country's second largest employer.

PROSPECT, APRIL 2007

Jews in Nice who want to buy a flat have to pay a fee of €900–7,000 to get around a Vichy law still on the books.

JERUSALEM POST, 1ST MARCH 2007

More than half of the London Underground network is over-ground.

PROSPECT RESEARCH

One of the stranger aspects of contemporary cricket in England is the toll it seems to take on players' mental health. *The suicide rate among cricketers is more than twice the British average, according to an article in the* **Spectator** *in March 2007*. But suicide is only the most obvious manifestation of the problem; former England opener Marcus Trescothick has given up international cricket, presumably because he doesn't want to deal with the stresses and strains associated with touring. When Trescothick abruptly decided to return home in the middle of England's 2006 Ashes tour in Australia, apparently suffering from depression, Geoffrey Boycott, a man not normally known for his public expressions of sympathy, wrote a *j'accuse* piece for the *Daily Telegraph*, blaming cricket's administrators for packing players' schedules with international games. Trescothick, he said, would not be the last England player to turn his back on his country.

21 per cent of the calories consumed by an average American come from beverages.

NEW YORK TIMES, 27TH MARCH 2007

In 1997, *Q*'s first free CD covermount increased sales of the magazine by 325 per cent.

BBC NEWS MAGAZINE, 13TH JULY 2007

In Britain, 25 per cent of the tobacco market is smuggled.

BRITISH AMERICAN TOBACCO

Half the primary carers of children in south Wales are men.

CLIVE SOLEY MP

Per capita, Australia emits 30 per cent more greenhouse gases
than the US.
ADAM SMITH INSTITUTE

Almost 1 per cent of Guatemalan children are adopted by
American families.
NEW YORK TIMES, 6TH NOVEMBER 2006

Phoenix, Arizona, is America's fifth largest city, with a
population of about 1.45m.
US CENSUS BUREAU

The Dutch smoke more than anyone in the developed world –
around one in three adults are regular smokers.
THE GUARDIAN, 30TH JULY 2005

The Irish drive an average 15,000 miles a year, more than
Americans and the British.
THE WEEK, 31ST DECEMBER 2004

Over 10 per cent of the Australian government's revenue comes
from gambling.
COMMENT IS FREE, 27TH MARCH 2007

8.5 per cent of American CEOs live on a golf course.
SAN JOSE MERCURY NEWS, 12TH APRIL 2007

Ants spend only one fifth of their day working.
'1,000 COMMON DELUSIONS' BY CHRISTA POPPELMANN

Only 3 per cent of male birds have a penis.
THE ECONOMIST, 5TH MAY 2007

Advertising wine is banned on French television.
BBC NEWS ONLINE, 27TH FEBRUARY 2007

There are twice as many privately owned tigers in America as there are in the wild across the world.

THE GUARDIAN, 2ND FEBRUARY 2007

By December 2005, the Afghan Cricket Federation had 12,000 members, up from 500 in 1995.

THE GUARDIAN, 10TH DECEMBER 2005

The suicide rate for 11–17 year olds is five times higher in Wales than England.

BBC NEWS ONLINE, 6TH FEBRUARY 2006

The IRS has a computer devoted solely to Bill Gates's tax return.

THE GUARDIAN, 11TH FEBRUARY 2006

Ireland is the second richest country in the OECD, behind Japan.

IRISH TIMES, 30TH JULY 2007

The 10 Downing Street door has always been black, except for a period during the premiership of Herbert Asquith (1908–16), when it was painted dark green.

DAILY TELEGRAPH, 2ND JUNE 2007

74 per cent of the women passengers aboard the *Titanic* survived, compared with 20 per cent of the men.

WEEKLY STANDARD, 10TH APRIL 2006

In 2004, the Texas Democratic party had no full-time staff.

NEW REPUBLIC, 13TH APRIL 2006

During a typical experiment, the Culham nuclear fusion plant in Oxfordshire consumes 2 per cent of the entire electricity capacity in Britain.

PROSPECT, JULY 2006

Of the 18 US presidents since 1900, only seven went, as undergraduates, to an Ivy League institution. Harry Truman never went to college at all.

TIMES LITERARY SUPPLEMENT, 12TH JULY 2006

Explosions from the battle of the Somme could be heard on Hampstead Heath.

'SOMME: THE HEROISM AND HORROR OF WAR' BY MARTIN GILBERT

Walt Disney was a direct 22nd-generation descendant of Edward I.

'ON ROYALTY' BY JEREMY PAXMAN

Parmesan cheese accounts for 10 per cent of thefts from Italian shops – more than any other good.

SUNDAY TELEGRAPH, 5TH NOVEMBER 2006

5 per cent of China's GDP is exported directly to Wal-Mart.

THE OBSERVER, 19TH DECEMBER 2004

One of the many difficulties in forging a new global deal on curbing global warming is that those countries with the most to lose from rising temperatures are in many cases not the same countries whose carbon dioxide emissions created the problem in the first place. Nevertheless, *in 2002, Bangladesh showed considerable foresight in becoming the first country to ban plastic bags*, as the *Guardian* reported in May 2007. Bangladesh is prone to regular flooding, and a rise in sea levels would obviously compound the problem – ironically, the ban was put in place because plastic bags were apparently clogging drains, leading to further flooding during the monsoon season.

There are 60 casinos in Moscow – more than any other city in the world bar Las Vegas and Miami.

WORLD CASINO DIRECTORY

One of Olivia Newton-John's grandfathers was Max Born, a Nobel-winning physicist and one of the founders of quantum mechanics.

THE DAILY DISH, 6TH NOVEMBER 2006

The five most philanthropic American states, relative to their own wealth, are Mississippi, Arkansas, Oklahoma, Louisiana and Alabama.

CATALOGUEFORPHILANTHROPY.ORG

In terms of population percentage, Australia sustained more losses in the first world war than any other nation.

'EVERYTHING YOU DIDN'T NEED TO KNOW ABOUT AUSTRALIA'
BY ADAM WARD

In 2001, the year of the foot and mouth epidemic, fewer animals
were culled or slaughtered than in an average year.

DAVID KING, FORMER CHIEF SCIENTIFIC ADVISER

Brussels's unemployment rate is 20 per cent.

FINANCIAL TIMES, 23RD DECEMBER 2007

When average disposable income is adjusted for the cost of
living, Scandinavians are the poorest people in western
Europe; the Spanish and the Portuguese are the richest.

KPMG

Women had the vote in Turkey before France, Italy, Switzerland
and Belgium.

FINANCIAL TIMES, 3RD OCTOBER 2005

Nearly half of America's 4m-plus Muslims are black. Only
one in eight is of Arab origin; 70 per cent of Arab-
Americans are Christian.

THE TIMES, 16TH AUGUST 2004

One of the fallouts from the run-up to the Iraq war was,
of course, the entrenchment of deep mutual distrust
between America and France. So it should come as no
surprise that a survey carried out in April 2007 by the
International Herald Tribune and the news channel France
24 found that 38 per cent of Americans said they had a
'negative opinion' of France – higher than the figure for
Britain, Italy, Germany or Spain. But there was one
country that exceeded the US in its dislike for France:
France. *44 per cent of French people told the pollsters
that they had a negative opinion of their own country.*
So it seems the surrender monkeys are not only cheese-
eating but self-hating too.

In 1990 the average age of video game players in Britain was 18; by 2004 it was 29.

THE OBSERVER, 1ST FEBRUARY 2004

In the 2000 US presidential election, the five richest states all voted for Al Gore, while George W Bush took the 14 poorest states (apart from New Mexico).

FINANCIAL TIMES, 24TH JULY 2004

Of the 3,633 deaths in the Northern Ireland Troubles, 2,139 were caused by the IRA, 1,050 by loyalist paramilitaries and 52 by the RUC.

'LOST LIVES' BY DAVID MCKITTRICK ET AL

It is possible to donate half a liver.

BBC

35 ministers in Harold Macmillan's government, including seven cabinet ministers, were related to him by marriage.

'A HISTORY OF MODERN BRITAIN' BY ANDREW MARR

By the late 1970s, Kingsley Amis was spending £1,000 a month on scotch.

BOOKFORUM, FEBRUARY/MARCH 2008

Bacteria of the species Pseudomonas fluorescens can go from a population of just 500 to 200m over the course of one night.

THE WILD SIDE, 25TH MARCH 2008

Ireland has 1m fewer inhabitants than in the 1850s.

PROSPECT, MAY 2008

In the last 200 years, France has taken in more immigrants than any other European country.

BLOOMBERG.COM, 26TH FEBRUARY 2008

Funny OLD words

Facts about our language and names

About 85 per cent of Chinese people share only 100 surnames. Wang is the most popular (93m), followed by Li (92m) and Zhang (88m). At least 100,000 people are called 'Wang Tao', making it the most popular full name.

CHINA DAILY, 12TH JUNE 2007

On a QWERTY keyboard, 32 per cent of keystrokes take place on the 'home' (middle) row, 52 per cent on the upper row and 16 per cent on the bottom row.

JARED DIAMOND

There are over 60 people with the first name 'Hitler' in Venezuela.

NEW YORK TIMES, 5TH SEPTEMBER 2007

In the Eskimo language Inuktitut, there is a single word meaning 'I should try not to become an alcoholic' – *Iminngernaveersaartunngortussaavunga.*

NEW YORK SUN, 28TH DECEMBER 2006

Paul Wolfowitz, formerly US deputy defence secretary and head of the World Bank, speaks French, German, Arabic, Hebrew and Indonesian.

NEW YORKER, 9TH APRIL 2007

The insults moron, idiot, imbecile and cretin were all once official medical diagnoses.

BALDERDASH & PIFFLE, BBC2

'Stewardesses' is the longest word typed with only the left hand and 'lollipop' with the right.

THE URBAN DICTIONARY

Counting up from zero, and excluding the word 'and', the first number to contain an 'a' is 'thousand'.

PROSPECT RESEARCH

Molly is the most popular name for both dogs and cats in
Britain.
YAHOO NEWS, 28TH MAY 2007

The 14th most popular search term entered into Google is
'Google'.
TIME, 6TH JUNE 2007

The term 'blockbuster' was coined in the 1920s, meaning a film
whose queue of customers at the box office was so long
that it could not be contained on a single city block.
WASHINGTON POST, 27TH FEBRUARY 2005

The words tomato, coyote, avocado and chocolate all come
from the Aztec language Nahuatl.
MARGINAL REVOLUTION, 27TH FEBRUARY 2006

The word 'bible' does not appear in the works of Shakespeare.

THE GUARDIAN, 3RD MARCH 2006

The five most-used nouns in the English language are time, person, year, way and day.

CNN, 22ND JUNE 2006

Drivers called Ben are most likely to crash their cars; Ians are the safest.

THE GUARDIAN, 8TH JULY 2006

Fidel Castro's fascination with Alexander the Great led him to name three of his sons Alexis, Alexander and Alejandro.

NEW YORKER, 31ST JULY 2006

The highest possible legal score on a first turn in Scrabble is given by the word 'muzjiks', giving 128 points. The world record for the highest score on a single turn is 'quixotry' (365 points).

WIKIPEDIA/SLATE, 26TH OCTOBER 2006

The collective noun for owls is 'parliament'.

WIKIPEDIA

No words in the English language rhyme with orange, silver, purple or month.

NEW SCIENTIST, 18TH DECEMBER 2004

Goethe's **Faust** is 12,111 lines long. The full text of *Hamlet* is 3,800 lines.

PROSPECT, JUNE 2001

The word 'boredom' did not exist in the English language until after 1750.

'BOREDOM: THE LITERARY HISTORY OF A STATE OF MIND'
BY PATRICIA M SPACKS

In mid-2004, Mohammed was the most popular name for
newborn boys in Amsterdam.

THE ATLANTIC, JUNE 2004

There is no word for 'please' in Gujarati.

NEW STATESMAN, 25TH JULY 2005

Shakespeare used a total of 31,534 different words in his works,
although 14,376 appeared only once.

PROSPECT, JULY 2004

Because Chinese number words are so brief, the average
Chinese speaker can hold nine digits in his or her
active memory at once, compared to seven for English
speakers.

NEW YORKER, 3RD MARCH 2008

There are 500,000 words in the *Oxford English Dictionary*.
French has less than a fifth of this number.

'THE DAY BRITAIN DIED' BY ANDREW MARR

The word 'queueing' is the only word in English with five
consecutive vowels.

PROSPECT RESEARCH

Nearly 3,500 Chinese children have been named after the
Olympics. Most of the children named Aoyun
(Mandarin for Olympics) are males born around 2000,
when China was bidding to host the games. Another
4,000 children share names with the Games mascots.

METRO, 5TH NOVEMBER 2007

The word 'paradise' comes from a Persian word meaning 'walled
around'.

'FENCING PARADISE' BY RICHARD MABEY

The 'zip' of zip code stands for 'zone improvement plan'.

CHICAGO TRIBUNE, 2ND DECEMBER 2002

An 18-year-old knows 60,000 words, a learning rate of one
word per 90 waking minutes from the age of one.

STEVEN PINKER

Egyptians, Indians and Turks search for 'sex' on Google more
than any other nationality. 'Hitler' is most popular in
Germany, Austria and Mexico; 'Nazi' in Chile, Australia
and Britain. 'David Beckham' gets most hits in
Venezuela.

REUTERS, 17TH OCTOBER 2007

By the age of five, children have acquired 85 per cent of the
language they will have as adults.

JOHN BASTIANI, RSA LECTURE

Marlboro cigarettes took their name from Great Marlborough
Street – the location of the Philip Morris factory that
first produced them.

LONDONIST.COM, 18TH FEBRUARY 2008

Of all the words in the *Oxford English Dictionary,* 99 per
cent derive from languages other than Old English.
However, words that derive from Old English make
up 62 per cent of the words most used.

'THE POWER OF BABEL' BY JOHN MCWHORTER

'Broadcast' is a term borrowed from farmers, describing what
they do with seeds across a field.

WEEKLY STANDARD, 14TH JUNE 2004

There are 823 languages spoken in Papua New Guinea, more
than any other country in the world.

'LIMITS OF LANGUAGE' BY MIKAEL PARKVALL

'*Lula*' – the Brazilian president's nickname – means 'squid' in
    Portuguese.

                      FORTUNE, 1ST NOVEMBER 2004

Harry S Truman had no middle name – his advisers insisted he
    insert an initial to gain credibility with voters.

            BBC MAGAZINE MONITOR, 1ST FEBRUARY 2008

Ghanaians are often named after the day of the week on which
    they were born. Kofi Annan was born on and named
    after Friday.

                CROSS-CULTURAL SOLUTIONS

Jack Kerouac typed at 100 words a minute.

               NEW YORKER, 9TH APRIL 2007

The first written Afrikaans was in Arabic script, not Roman.

                PROSPECT, MAY 2004

The Finnish language has no future tense.

WIKIPEDIA

Mao Zedong had a hairdresser called Big Beard Wang.

THE AGE, 26TH AUGUST 2006

Over just six days in August 1998, the *Washington Post* devoted 80,289 words to the Monica Lewinsky scandal.

NEW REPUBLIC, 7TH SEPTEMBER 1998

Adult 'paradoxical frogs', which are found in the Amazon and Trinidad, are so named because they are a third of the size of their tadpoles.

ENCARTA CONCISE ENGLISH DICTIONARY

The 18th-century scholar Edmond Malone calculated that 4,144 of the 6,033 lines in parts I, II and III of *Henry VI* were plagiarised by Shakespeare.

'EX LIBRIS' BY ANNE FADIMAN

In 1982, a law was passed in Zimbabwe banning jokes about President Canaan Banana's name.

THE ECONOMIST, 29TH NOVEMBER 2003

The condition of being unable to release a dart from one's hand when throwing is known as 'dartitis'.

PROSPECT RESEARCH

There are no plurals in Chinese.

WIRED, DECEMBER 2006

Of almost 3,000 public schools in Florida, five are named after George Washington, compared with 11 named after manatees (sea mammals).

'WHAT'S IN A NAME?': THE DECLINE IN THE CIVIC MISSION OF SCHOOL NAMES'
BY JAY P GREENE, BRIAN KISIDA AND JONATHAN BUTCHER

Reasons to be Cheerful

Facts that might get you out of bed again

80 per cent of women and 78 per cent of men with cash assets over £500,000 say that money has brought them greater happiness.

SUNDAY TELEGRAPH, 8TH JULY 2007

Over 90 per cent of people who attempted to jump off the Golden Gate bridge but were stopped are either still alive or died of natural causes.

'WHERE ARE THEY NOW? A FOLLOW-UP STUDY OF SUICIDE ATTEMPTERS FROM THE GOLDEN GATE BRIDGE'

A pedestrian inside Paris's '75' postal code is never more than 500 metres from a Metro station.

INTERNATIONAL HERALD TRIBUNE, 18TH JUNE 2007

British families spend as much time eating together today as they did in the 1970s.

ECONOMIC AND SOCIAL RESEARCH COUNCIL

Despite its oil reserves, 99 per cent of Norway's electricity is produced by hydroelectric sources.

ENCARTA

From 1997 to 2005, the percentage of British men working more than 50 hours a week declined from 22 per cent to 16 per cent.

THE TIMES, 25TH APRIL 2007

In 2006, more women (244) than men (234) were ordained as clergy in the Church of England for the first time since the introduction of women priests in 1994.

THE GUARDIAN, 14TH NOVEMBER 2007

Kabul's population has increased from 300,000 in 2001 to 3m today.

FINANCIAL TIMES, 11TH FEBRUARY 2008

In 1987, 61 per cent of Britain's top lawyers, doctors, businessmen, politicians and journalists had attended Oxford or Cambridge University. In 2007, the figure had fallen to 47 per cent.

BRITISH COUNCIL

In 2006, there were 77 major commercial plane crashes worldwide, the lowest number ever recorded. Only 20 involved fatalities.

FOREIGN POLICY, NOVEMBER/DECEMBER 2007

Only one British circus keeps big cats, and fewer than 50 wild animals perform in four British-owned circuses (including seven tigers, eight camels, five lions, several zebras and a retired elephant called Anne who tours but no longer performs).

BBC NEWS ONLINE, 7TH DECEMBER 2007

In Britain in 1966, there were 86,700 births to women under 20; by 2003, this number had fallen to 44,200.

SPIKED ONLINE, 26TH MAY 2005

Since 1990, the average American has added about two and a half years to his life, but the average New Yorker has added 6.2 years. In the year 2004 alone, New Yorkers' life expectancy shot up by five months.

NEW YORK MAGAZINE, 20TH AUGUST 2007

In India, 127m people were vaccinated against polio in a single day in 1997.

WORLD HEALTH ORGANISATION

In 2005, 71 per cent of email users said they had received pornographic email spam. In 2007 the number was 52 per cent.

PEW RESEARCH CENTRE

In the US, in 1950 the ratio of workers to retirees was 18 to 1. In 2050, it is projected to be 2 to 1. But in 2050 the worker to dependent ratio will be 10 to 8 – better than in the 1960s, when it was 10 to 9.

PROSPECT, FEBRUARY 2008

In Britain, there are fewer police trained in the use of arms than there were 30 years ago.

RADIO 5 LIVE, 16TH MAY 2006

Between 1989 and 2005, the number of incidences of mass killing of civilians around the world decreased by 90 per cent.

NEW REPUBLIC, 22ND MARCH 2007

August 2006 marked one thousand days of peace between nations – the longest period since the second world war.

CHRISTIAN SCIENCE MONITOR, 30TH AUGUST 2006

Over 90 per cent of aeroplane crashes have survivors.

BBC NEWS ONLINE, 3RD OCTOBER 2006

Cumbria has the lowest number of homicides in England and Wales – none in 2007 compared to 168 in London.

HOME OFFICE

In 1895, 5 per cent of Britain was covered in woodland; by 2003 the figure was 11.8 per cent.

THE OBSERVER, 26TH JANUARY 2003

In December 2006, 65 per cent of Iranians had a very unfavourable view of the US. By April 2008, this had fallen to 51 per cent.

WORLDPUBLICOPINION.ORG

The decline in crime in New York City over the last 15 years or so is well known, but the sheer scale of the drop still gives pause for thought. *In 2007, there were 494 homicides in New York – by far the lowest number in a 12-month period since 1963.* Of course, the figure is still high by British standards – between April 2006 and March 2007 there were just 168 homicides in London, whose population is only slightly smaller than New York's. But London's figures have stayed roughly stable over the last few years, while New York's continue to fall.

In the US in 2003, the total number of cancer deaths dropped for the first time since records began in 1930. The biggest cause was a decline in the number of smokers.

NEW SCIENTIST, 18TH FEBRUARY 2006

Between 1962 and 2002, life expectancy in the middle east and north Africa increased from around 48 years to 69 – the strongest performance of any region in the world.

CHARLES KENNY

The fertility rate in the US – 2.1 children per woman – is the highest it has been for 35 years.

NEW YORK TIMES, 1ST FEBRUARY 2008

In Britain, under-25s save more as a percentage of their income than any other age group.

THE GUARDIAN, 2ND MARCH 2005

In the US in 1940, 58 per cent of black women with jobs worked as maids. Now only 1 per cent do.

THE ECONOMIST, 4TH AUGUST 2005

Since decentralising its energy in 1992, Woking has cut its carbon dioxide emissions by 77 per cent.

THE TIMES, 2ND NOVEMBER 2006

The proportion of people in developing countries living in absolute poverty decreased from 29 per cent in 1990 to 18 per cent in 2004.

WORLD BANK

In the six London boroughs affected by the July 2005 bombings and attempted bombings, crime in July fell by 12 per cent compared to July 2004.

THE ECONOMIST, 27TH AUGUST 2005

The number of attempted bank and building society robberies in Britain fell from 1,400 in 1991 to 250 in 2003.

THE ECONOMIST, 3RD JANUARY 2004

Three quarters of the 35,000 appeals against congestion charge penalty notices made by London drivers have been successful.

THE GUARDIAN, 14TH FEBRUARY 2004

In 1971, a third of Britons over 16 had no teeth; by 2004 this had fallen to just 12 per cent.

THE TIMES, 1ST APRIL 2004

80 per cent of British companies have a website – more than any other country in the world.

RTC NORTH FORESIGHT

During the war in Bosnia, Germany took in 350,000 Bosnian refugees.

GERMAN GOVERNMENT

Nick Drake sold only 4,000 albums during his lifetime. Since his death in 1974, sales have reached nearly 1m.

CHANNEL 4 NEWS, 21ST MAY 2004

In the US, the teenage birth rate hit an all-time low in 2005, at 21 per 1,000 young women aged 15 to 17.

NEW YORK TIMES, 13TH JULY 2007

Passengers near the tail of a plane are about 40 per cent more likely to survive a crash than those in the first few rows up front.

POPULAR MECHANICS, 18TH JULY 2007

The number of armed conflicts in the world has declined by more than 40 per cent since 1992.

HUMAN SECURITY REPORT 2005

Suicide is always a tragedy, so the fact that *England's suicide rate is at its lowest since records began,* as reported by the *Daily Telegraph* in April 2006, is obviously good news. Yet the causes of the drop are oddly prosaic: the withdrawal from sale of the painkiller co-proxamol, commonly used in suicides; the replacement of toxic coal gas with natural gas in the late 1960s, which made sticking one's head in an oven 'obsolete'; and the rise of the catalytic converter in the 1990s, which by removing carbon monoxide from car exhaust fumes put a stop to the favoured suicide method of the middle-aged suburban male. As with any economic good, when the 'costs' of committing suicide rise, 'demand' falls. This fact is comforting in that it suggests that further falls in the rate may be relatively simple to achieve through straightforward technical measures, but it also conceals a tragic thought: that thousands of suicides over the past century were easily avoided.

There are now nearly as many American Indians in California as there were in the 18th century.

NEW YORK REVIEW OF BOOKS, 7TH OCTOBER 2004

In Britain, half of all appeals against parking tickets are successful, yet only 1 per cent of tickets are appealed against.

THE TIMES, 27TH MARCH 2008

In 1990, only 19 companies from the developing world made the Fortune top 500 list of global firms. In 2005, this had risen to 47.

WILSON QUARTERLY, SPRING 2008

On average, London's commuters get wet just 12 times a year.

TRANSPORT FOR LONDON

86 per cent of fathers attend the birth of their children.

FATHERHOOD INSTITUTE

Cuba will lift its ban on toasters in 2010.

NEW YORK TIMES, 14TH MARCH 2008

60 per cent of all Porsches ever built are still on the road.

PORSCHE

Cycling in London has risen by 83 per cent since 2000. Yet over the past decade, the numbers of cyclists killed or seriously injured on the road has fallen by a third.

THE ECONOMIST, 26TH APRIL 2008

STORIES

Facts that tell a mini-story in themselves

Michelin recently launched a guide to Tokyo dining. It awarded more stars to restaurants in the Japanese capital (191) than to any other city in the world. Paris gets 64 and New York 42.

FINANCIAL TIMES, 19TH NOVEMBER 2007

44 per cent of the British population still live within the local authority in which they were born. But only 12 per cent of graduates do.

PERFORMANCE AND INNOVATION UNIT

At the beginning of the Troubles, 20 per cent of Ulster Protestants described themselves as Irish. Today 3 per cent do.

ARTHUR AUGHEY, UNIVERSITY OF ULSTER

By 2004, Britain was the only major country in the world in which French was the main foreign language taught in schools.

THE TIMES, 8TH APRIL 2004

35 per cent of US and 20 per cent of British entrepreneurs are dyslexic. But only 1 per cent of corporate managers in the US have dyslexia.

NEW YORK TIMES, 6TH DECEMBER 2007

Mathematics and computer sciences have the highest university dropout rate in Britain, with one in ten undergraduates not continuing into a second year of study. Medicine and dentistry have the highest retention rate (98 per cent).

COMPUTING, 2ND AUGUST 2007

In 2007, total European stock market capitalisation exceeded that of the US for the first time since 1945.

PAUL KENNEDY LECTURE, LSE, 6TH FEBRUARY 2008

Americans are well known for developing personal obses-
sions with foreign 'ancestries' that may actually date back
several hundred years. But as the country ages, it may be
starting to develop a more confident attitude towards its
own history. In October 2004, the *Atlantic* magazine dis-
cussed a recent report from the US Census Bureau,
which had asked Americans to identify their 'ancestral
identity'. 43m Americans said German, making it, perhaps surprisingly, the most popular answer. 32m said
Irish, and 25m each African-American and English. But
most revealingly, *the fastest growing identity was 'American', the term chosen by 20m – up by 8m since the early
1990s.*

At a Republican party convention in mid-2007, it cost $5,000
to pose for a photo with President Bush. In summer
2006, officials charged at least $10,000, and in the 2000
and 2004 campaigns, a Bush photo-op commanded
$25,000.
HUFFINGTON POST, 4TH JUNE 2007

53 per cent of births in London are to immigrant mothers.
In Kensington and Chelsea the figure is 68 per cent.
NEWSWEEK, 6TH AUGUST 2007

An estimated 10 per cent of CDs produced in Britain are
covermounts.
BBC NEWS MAGAZINE, 13TH JULY 2007

In 1976, the US had 30 per cent of the world's college students.
By 2006, that had dropped to 14 per cent.
BUSINESS REPORT, 25TH JUNE 2007

The second half of the 20th century saw western women enter the workforce in unprecedented numbers, and the military was no exception. The proportion of female troops killed in America's various wars throughout the period, as documented by *Slate* in December 2001, tells its own story. Of the 36,568 Americans killed in the Korean war, two were women – 0.005 per cent. In Vietnam, eight out of the 58,204 who died were female – 0.01 per cent. *In the Gulf war, when 383 Americans were killed, 15 were women – 3.9 per cent. Interestingly, however, at the time of writing, of the 4,000 US troops killed in Iraq since the 2003 invasion, 95 have been women – a slight drop to 2.4 per cent.* A setback for the sisterhood? Perhaps, but it's difficult to imagine anyone losing any sleep over it. And moreover, women now make up around 15 per cent of active duty forces, a fourfold rise since 1991.

23 per cent of plastic bags used in Britain are from Tesco.

BBC

In 1995, the US won 51 per cent of the votes in the UN general assembly; by 2006, the figure had fallen to just 24 per cent.

'WHAT DOES CHINA THINK?' BY MARK LEONARD

By 15, only half of American children live with both biological parents, compared with roughly two thirds of Swedish, German and French children, and 90 per cent of children in Spain and Italy.

AMERICAN PROSPECT, JUNE 2005

China owns no aircraft carriers.

REAL CLEAR POLITICS, 28TH MAY 2007

In the first quarter of 2007, at least 128m internet domain
names were registered worldwide, a 31 per cent
increase over the previous year.

INTERNATIONAL HERALD TRIBUNE, 23RD JULY 2007

Britain spends about £38 per head a year on legal aid, compared
to £4 in Germany and £3 in France.

THE GUARDIAN, 10TH JANUARY 2008

27.5 per cent of first degree graduates in Northern Ireland stay
in education or training after graduating – the highest
figure in Britain.

OFFICE FOR NATIONAL STATISTICS

Doubling the number of engineering students in the US would
increase GDP by 0.5 per cent, while the same change in
the number studying law would cause a 0.3 per cent
drop.

'THE STATE TO COME' BY WILL HUTTON

More Ethiopian doctors are practising in Chicago than
in Ethiopia.

THE ECONOMIST, 13TH JULY 2005

Ten years after graduation, 44 per cent of 1980 female Harvard
graduates who had married kept their own name, while
just 32 per cent of 1990 graduates kept theirs.

HARVARD GAZETTE, 26TH AUGUST 2004

Only 13 per cent of Japanese homes have ever been resold,
compared to 89 per cent in Britain and 78 per cent
in the US.

THE ECONOMIST, 3RD JANUARY 2008

80 per cent of British fathers think of Christmas as a
'relaxing holiday break'; only 35 per cent of
mothers share this view.

'HAVING NONE OF IT' BY SUZANNE FRANKS

More than half of Indians go online before leaving the house,
while less than one third of Americans or Canadians do.

BUSINESS WEEK, 10TH MAY 2007

41 per cent of female Scottish graduates are still childless
between the ages of 45 and 49, compared with under
30 per cent south of the border.

GLASGOW HERALD, 29TH JUNE 2004

During the 1950s, 20 per cent of Americans changed residence
every year and 6.9 per cent moved across county
borders. During the 1990s, the comparable figures
were 17 per cent and 6.6 per cent.

PROSPECT RESEARCH

An average 1,500 immigrants a day enter Britain planning to
stay for a year or more.

OFFICE FOR NATIONAL STATISTICS

43 per cent of Americans approve of using gene therapy to
enhance the physical and behavioural traits of children,
as well as to resolve genetic diseases.

PEW RESEARCH CENTRE

Number of people killed per minute in the four Rambo films:
Rambo: First Blood (1982): 0.01; *Rambo: First Blood
Part II* (1985): 0.72; *Rambo III* (1988): 1.30; *Rambo IV*
(2008): 2.59

MARGINAL REVOLUTION, 21ST JANUARY 2008

During the 2005 riots in France, 33 per cent of those questioned by the police were European in origin, 36 per cent were north African and 29 per cent sub-Saharan African.

DISSENT, SUMMER 2006

Four of the five richest Americans – Bill Gates, casino owner Sheldon Adelson, Oracle's Larry Ellison and Microsoft co-founder Paul Allen – are college dropouts. (The exception is Warren Buffett.)

'ALL THE MONEY IN THE WORLD: HOW THE FORBES 400 MAKE – AND SPEND – THEIR FORTUNES' BY PETER W BERNSTEIN AND ANNALYN SWAN

Twin births in Britain have increased from 1 in 98 in 1983 to 1 in 68 in 2003.

THE SPECTATOR, 1ST OCTOBER 2005

There are at least 700 9/11 memorials in New York city.

HARPER'S, JANUARY 2008

In 1914, Britain had nine ambassadors. Today there are roughly 140 ambassadors plus nine accredited to multilateral organisations.

PROSPECT RESEARCH

Most adults in London are unmarried, including 80 per cent of those aged under 30. In every other large British city and county, at least 55 per cent of people aged 16 and over are married.

JOSEPH ROWNTREE FOUNDATION

In 1949, there were 160,000 Young Conservatives; by 1997, there were 3,000.

'BLUE SKIES AHEAD', CENTRE FOR POLICY STUDIES

Between a third and half of the developing world's science and technology workers live in the west.

IPPR

In 1882, there were 268 'designated ancient monuments' in Britain. Today there are 12,900.

'THEATRES OF MEMORY' BY RAPHAEL SAMUEL

The US grants 78 per cent more high-tech patents per capita than Europe.

TIME, 19TH JANUARY 2004

In 2005, the number of English families with second homes passed 500,000 for the first time – a rise of 10 per cent in a year. Of the almost 330,000 second homes owned in Britain, nearly 80,000 are in Devon or Cornwall.

THE GUARDIAN, 21ST FEBRUARY 2006

The rapid rise of the mobile phone is probably the most significant technology story of the past 20 years, and yes, that includes the internet. While computers, let alone networked communications, remain unknown in many parts of the globe, much of the developing world has embraced mobile communications technology. Lacking the necessary infrastructure for widespread adoption of fixed landlines, they have 'leapfrogged' straight to mobiles. In Africa, where landline coverage is patchiest, the number of mobile phone users overtook the number of landline users in 2001. And now the world has gone mobile – *in early 2008, AP reported that in the course of the year, the number of mobile phone users would overtake the number of non-users*. To understand the scale of this shift, consider that just eight years earlier, only 12 per cent of the world's population had a handset.

31 per cent of practising doctors in Britain were trained abroad, compared to 5 per cent in France and Germany.

THE LANCET, 27TH MAY 2005

In 1995 there were 225 television programmes in Britain watched by more than 15m people. In 2004, there were just ten.

JACK STRAW

In 2000, for the first time in more than 200 years, more babies were born in France than in any other European country.

'OLD EUROPE? DEMOGRAPHIC CHANGE AND PENSION REFORM' BY DAVID WILLETTS, CENTRE FOR EUROPEAN REFORM

> *The lord chancellor has used his power to sack a judge
> only twice since the Act of Settlement in 1701*, according
> to the *Daily Telegraph* in 2006. In 1830, Jonah Barrington
> was dismissed for stealing the money that litigants paid
> into court. And in 1983, former Conservative MP Bruce
> Campbell was fired from the judiciary after being caught
> smuggling 125 litres of whisky and 9,000 cigarettes into
> Britain on his private yacht. Campbell could have retired:
> he opted for dismissal only because a legal anomaly
> meant he kept his pension. In 1990, Campbell died in
> Canterbury.

In 2000, there were 150 people working at 10 Downing Street,
compared with over 1,000 in the prime minister's
departments of both Canada and Australia.

'THE BRITISH CONSTITUTION IN THE TWENTIETH CENTURY'
EDITED BY VERNON BOGDANOR

In 2002, white men comprised 44 per cent of the British
population but only 26 per cent of medical students.

THE TIMES, 3RD SEPTEMBER 2004

Between 2000 and 2005, the number of people in the US
playing golf more than 25 times a year fell by a third,
from 6.9m to 4.5m.

NEW YORK TIMES, 21ST FEBRUARY 2008

In 2005, 206,000 books were published in Britain – a rise of 28
per cent over 2004, and more than the US, where the
number fell 18,000 to 172,000.

BOWKER

In 40 per cent of weddings in Britain in 2005, at least one
person was getting married for at least the second time.

THE OBSERVER, 3RD FEBRUARY 2008

John Kerry was only the third Catholic to stand for the US
presidency, after Al Smith in 1928 and JFK in 1960.

INTERNATIONAL HERALD TRIBUNE, 11TH MAY 2004

In 2007, Harvard accepted only 9 per cent of undergraduate
applicants, the lowest figure in its history, down from
18 per cent in 1983.

REASON, 21ST MAY 2007

In 2004, only three European countries had laws against
'apologie' for or 'glorification' of terrorism. By
November 2006, 36 countries had committed to
criminalising the 'provocation' of terrorism.

HUMAN RIGHTS WATCH WORLD REPORT, 2007

20 per cent of British households have dishwashers, compared
to 35 per cent in continental Europe and 55 per cent in
the US.

PROCTER & GAMBLE NEWS

In 2006 in the US, sales of hip hop albums fell by 33 per cent –
twice as much as the decline in CD sales overall.

DAILY TELEGRAPH, 2ND JULY 2007

In California, 30 per cent of newborn black female babies are
given names unique among all newborns in the state
that year.

SLATE, 11TH APRIL 2005

The US population reached 100m in 1915, 200m in 1967 and
300m in 2006.

NEW YORK TIMES, 13TH JANUARY 2006

67 per cent of Britons think there are too many legal immigrants living in their country; 20 per cent think the number is about right. In contrast, 32 per cent of the French think there are too many and 52 per cent think the number is about right.

INTERNATIONAL HERALD TRIBUNE, 24TH MAY 2007

In Chicago and New York, among other US cities, full-time female employees in their 20s earn more on average than males.

QUEENS COLLEGE, NEW YORK

In early 2007, the proportion of French people who described themselves as Catholic was 51 per cent, down from 62 per cent in just four years.

THE INDEPENDENT, 22ND JANUARY 2007

There were 463 cars for every 1,000 Britons in 2004, compared with 581 in Italy, 550 in Germany and 503 in France.

THE TIMES, 31ST MARCH 2007

In the US, 45 per cent of Republicans say they are happy compared to 29 per cent of Democrats.

PEW RESEARCH CENTRE

Over the past five years, 2.9m rooms have been 'lost' in British homes as a result of open-plan conversions.

DAILY MIRROR, 29TH JANUARY 2008

In 1981, 24 per cent of British mothers returned to work within a year of giving birth; 20 years later, the figure was 67 per cent.

THE GUARDIAN, 6TH DECEMBER 2004

The phenomenal growth of Ireland over the past 30 years or so has turned a poor outpost of western Europe into one of the most vibrant economies in the world – one whose per capita income is now significantly higher than Britain's. But with economic success, of course, comes a new set of challenges, particularly immigration; Ireland, of course, is better known for its exports rather than imports of workers (in the US alone, 32m people claim Irish ancestry – almost nine times the population of Ireland itself). What's also striking is the speed with which the numbers can turn themselves around – *back in 1998, the* **International Herald Tribune** *reported that while Ireland had seen a net 200,000 people emigrate during the 1980s, between April 1996 and 1997, 15,000 more people arrived than left.* Now Ireland is home to around 420,000 foreign nationals – around 10 per cent of the population.

In the 1951 British general election, more than 200 MPs were elected by over 50 per cent of their constituency electorate. In 2001, none were.

'THE POINT OF DEPARTURE' BY ROBIN COOK

In the eight years after the end of the cold war, 504 resolutions were put before the UN security council. During the previous 45 years there were 659.

ALAN MUNRO

In the first six months of 2007, non-Britons were charged with 22,793 crimes in London. Poles accounted for 2,310 of these – more than any other nationality.

THE OBSERVER, 7TH OCTOBER 2007

Manchester United is the seventh most hated brand in the world, whereas Chelsea is only 29th (but up from 72 in 2006).

THE GUARDIAN, 7TH MAY 2007

44 per cent of Scots, 36 per cent of Londoners and 32 per cent of Mancunians have never set foot in a farmyard. However, 85 per cent of people from southwest England and 81 per cent of East Anglians have.

BBC NEWS, 8TH JUNE 2007

Moscow has a Muslim population of about 2.5m – the largest of any European city. Since 1989, Russia's Muslim population has increased by 40 per cent to about 25m.

SAN FRANCISCO CHRONICLE, 19TH NOVEMBER 2006

In 1820 China and India contributed nearly half of the world's income; by 1950 their share had fallen to less than a tenth. Today it is just less than a fifth.

BOSTON REVIEW, JANUARY/FEBRUARY 2008

Not a single enterprise founded in France in the past 40 years has managed to break into the ranks of the 25 biggest French companies. By comparison, 19 of today's 25 largest US companies didn't exist four decades ago.

WASHINGTON POST, 5TH JUNE 2005

Of the Nobel prizes awarded between 1951 and 2000, Jews won 32 per cent of awards for medicine, 32 per cent for physics, 30 per cent for economics and 29 per cent of all awards for science. Jews make up less than 0.5 per cent of the world's population.

'HUMAN ACCOMPLISHMENT' BY CHARLES MURRAY

When the channel tunnel opened in 1994, 15.9m annual Eurostar passengers were forecast. The actual number was 18 per cent of that – 2.9m. In 2001, passenger numbers were 6.9m.

'MEGAPROJECTS AND RISK' BY BENT FLYVBJERG

20 per cent of London houses sold for over $10m are bought by Russians. For those over $30m, the figure is 50 per cent.

NEW REPUBLIC, 2ND APRIL 2007

In Germany, only 13.5 per cent of children under three attend nursery schools, compared with the European average of 35 per cent.

EXPATICA, 15TH MAY 2007

On average, Americans are more than four times as likely to move house over a year than the Japanese.

SLATE, 18TH JULY 2005

In 2006, Britons spent £497m on cosmetic surgery – more than any other European country.

BBC NEWS ONLINE, 15TH FEBRUARY 2008

The average company report to shareholders among the 350 largest London-listed companies is nearly 140 pages, twice as long as ten years ago.

ECONOMIST.COM, 18TH DECEMBER 2007

The average American lives 13 years longer than the average celebrity, who is four times as likely to commit suicide.

TIME.COM

By May 2007, Latin was taught at 459 of Britain's 4,000 state secondary schools, up from 200 in 2003.

DAILY TELEGRAPH, 14TH MAY 2007

By late 2006, only 35 per cent of Americans had sent a text
  message, compared to almost 100 per cent in Britain.

MIT TECHNOLOGY REVIEW, 6TH NOVEMBER 2006

In 2006, out of 190,000 serving men and women in the British
  armed forces, fewer than 300 – 0.16 per cent – were
  Muslim. So the proportion of Muslims in the British
  population – 3 per cent – is about 20 times as high as
  it is in the armed forces.

PROSPECT RESEARCH

Over 50 per cent of parents of children at private schools were
  themselves state-educated.

SUTTON TRUST

Paper consumption in the US rose by an average 5.7 per cent a
  year between 1985 and 1999. Since then it has fallen by
  0.9 per cent annually.

CROOKED TIMBER, 23RD JUNE 2007

The last women's studies undergraduate course, at London
  Metropolitan University, closed in summer 2008.

TIMES HIGHER EDUCATION

In Britain, transaction costs amount to an average 2 per cent
  of house purchase prices. In Belgium, the figure is 18
  per cent.

FINANCIAL TIMES, 5TH NOVEMBER 2004

Since 1980, the population of the 'greater middle east' (30
  mainly Muslim countries from Morocco in the west to
  Bangladesh in the east) has nearly doubled, from 350m
  to 600m, while its share of world exports has fallen
  from 13.5 per cent to 4 per cent.

PROGRESSIVE POLICY INSTITUTE

Ever since the mid-19th century, intellectuals have been sounding the death knell for religion, arguing that the rise of science and the power of reason leaves no room for claims about the world based on faith rather than evidence. Yet it seems that God – or the gods – is not only surviving, he's thriving. In November 2007, the *Economist* reported that *the proportion of the world's population that was attached to one of the four biggest religions – Christianity, Islam, Buddhism and Hinduism – had risen from 67 per cent in 1900 to 73 per cent in 2005.* And the word(s) is still being spread – in May 2007 *Foreign Policy* magazine wrote that Christianity, Hinduism and Islam had all grown at over 1 per cent between 2000 and 2005, along with smaller faiths like the Sikhs, the Bahais and the Jains.

Protestants make up 15 per cent of the population of Latin America – up from 3 per cent in just ten years. The Catholic proportion has dropped from 80 to 70 per cent.

THE ECONOMIST, 29TH OCTOBER 2005

Since 1991, 1.5m people have emigrated from east Germany – over two thirds of them women.

BERLIN INSTITUTE FOR POPULATION AND DEVELOPMENT

The Clintons sent 400,000 Christmas cards in 2000. In their first year in office, Laura and George W Bush sent 875,000. In 2002 they sent 1m, in 2003 1.3m and in 2004 2m.

INTERNATIONAL HERALD TRIBUNE, 13TH DECEMBER 2004

The nine highest-paying jobs in the US are in the medical
profession. Anaesthesiologists are the highest paid
(with a mean annual salary of $184,340), with surgeons
second. The only non-medical occupations in the top
15 are chief executives (ten) and airline pilots (14).
Lawyers are 16th highest. Restaurant worker is the
worst paid job, with a mean annual salary of $15,930.

FORBES, 4TH JUNE 2007

The total value of global mergers and acquisitions in 2006 was
$3,861bn – as recently as 1995 it was just $850bn.

FINANCIAL TIMES, 19TH JUNE 2007

The average American uses over nine times more water per year
than the average Briton – 1,870 cubic metres compared
to 205 cubic metres.

WORLD BANK

The ratio of espresso machines to population in Australia and
New Zealand is approximately 850 people to 1 machine,
only bested by Italy. In the US, there are roughly
20,000 people per espresso machine.

COFFEEGEEK.COM, 12TH JUNE 2007

The length of time from invention to application of the
ballpoint pen was 58 years; for the zip fastener it was
32 years.

DEPARTMENT FOR TRADE AND INDUSTRY

The US is home to 4 per cent of the global population aged
5–25, but accounts for more than a quarter of the global
public education budget. It spends as much as the
middle east, central and eastern Europe, central Asia,
Latin America, the Caribbean, south and west Asia
and sub-Saharan Africa combined.

UNESCO

When Pope John Paul II was elected in 1978, the Holy See had full ties with 85 states worldwide. When he died, the figure was 174.

THE ECONOMIST, 19TH JULY 2007

Brent, in north London, is the only place in Britain where women earn as much as men on average. Copeland (home of Sellafield) in Cumbria has the poorest women compared to men.

PROPERTYFINDER

The average size of women's breasts in Britain has increased from a 34B in the 1950s to a 36C today.

JANICE MEE, DE MONTFORT UNIVERSITY

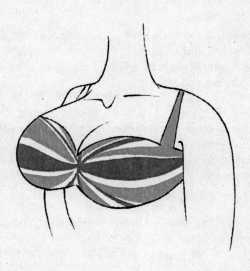

What's happened to Nessie? *In September 2007, the* **Times** *reported that there had been only two reported sightings of the Loch Ness monster so far that year, and that there had been only three in 2006.* A decade ago the numbers were consistently in the high teens. One theory is that the spread of digital cameras and camera phones makes it much more difficult to report sightings. After all, these days, any claim to have seen the Loch Ness monster – or, for that matter, the Yeti, Bigfoot, the Beast of Bodmin or googly-eyed extraterrestrial beings – will be met with the response, 'So did you get a picture?' If we assume that there is usually something questionable about such claims, then of course no photo will be forthcoming – in which case, why not spare yourself the embarrassment?

Indians account for 36 per cent of scientists at Nasa, 38 per cent of doctors in the US, and 34 per cent of employees at Microsoft, 28 per cent at IBM, 17 per cent at Intel and 13 per cent at Xerox.

THE TIMES OF INDIA, 11TH MARCH 2008

There are 14 countries in which there are more mobile phone subscriptions than there are people. The highest is Luxembourg, where there are 157 subscribers for every 100 people.

OECD

Women earn 57 per cent of bachelor's degrees and 59 per cent of master's degrees in the US, and a majority of research PhDs, but only 24 per cent of PhDs in the physical sciences.

THE SURVEY OF EARNED DOCTORATES

In 1968, France had 605,000 university students – as many as
Britain, West Germany and Belgium combined.

THE INDEPENDENT MAGAZINE, 23RD FEBRUARY 2008

Islam has overtaken Catholicism as the biggest religious
denomination in the world. Muslims make up
19.2 per cent of the world's population and Catholics
17.4 per cent.

REUTERS, 30TH MARCH 2008

There are 121 postcode areas in Britain. Since May 2008,
when Tesco opened branches in the Western Isles,
the Orkneys and Shetlands, the only one of these
areas without a Tesco has been Harrogate.

DAILY TELEGRAPH, 28TH MARCH 2008

House prices in Shanghai rose by 35 per cent in 2007.
Declines were biggest in the US (9 per cent) and
Ireland (7 per cent).

GLOBAL PROPERTY GUIDE

China became a net importer of coal in January 2007.

AGENCE FRANCE-PRESSE

In the US, in 2005, one third of wives outearned their
husbands.

WALL STREET JOURNAL, 1ST APRIL 2008

Since 2002, petrol stations in Britain have been shutting at an
average rate of 600 a year. There are now fewer people
selling fuel to motorists than at any time since 1912.

BBC NEWS ONLINE

44 per cent of churchgoers in London are black, compared
to 11 per cent of the city's population.

PROSPECT RESEARCH

In the US, women with MBAs are twice as likely to get divorced or separated as their male counterparts. (12 per cent of women with MBAs are divorced or separated compared with 5 per cent of men.)

WALL STREET JOURNAL, 1ST APRIL 2008

Almost 40 per cent of serving and former US military officials favour reinstating the draft to meet the recruitment crisis, almost twice as many as those who support allowing gays and lesbians to serve openly.

FOREIGN POLICY, MARCH/APRIL 2008

Inner London is the richest region in the EU. The EU's poorest region, at 24 per cent of the average, is northeastern Romania.

THE GUARDIAN, 12TH FEBRUARY 2008

and CURIOUSER CURIOUSER

Facts you didn't know you wanted to know

In the 1964 US presidential election, the Republican Barry Goldwater was given a hammering by President Lyndon Johnson. Yet many analysts credit Goldwater with revitalising the American conservative movement and, ultimately, paving the way for Ronald Reagan's election victories in the 1980s. For one conservative, however, the consequences were not so happy, as the *Times* reported in December 2005. Following the 1964 defeat, Karl Hess, Goldwater's chief speechwriter, looked for a new job. *After being rejected by every senator and congressman he approached, he applied to become the Senate lift attendant.* When this failed, he went on a welding course and took a job on the night shift in a machine shop.

71 per cent of dead people in Britain are cremated, but in Ireland the figure is only 5 per cent.

PROSPECT, APRIL 2003

Albert Einstein is the fifth highest earning dead celebrity, earning $18m in 2006 from use of his trademarked name on the Disney-owned 'Baby Einstein' brand of videos and toys. Royalties go to Jerusalem's Hebrew University, which was bequeathed the estate.

FORBES.COM, 29TH OCTOBER 2007

Britain has 13 times as many chartered accountants per capita as Germany.

PROSPECT RESEARCH

During the first world war, it cost the Entente powers £26,807 to kill an enemy soldier, while it cost the Central powers just £8,212.

'THE PITY OF WAR' BY NIALL FERGUSON

Tony Blair was the first sitting prime minister to visit California.
THE GUARDIAN, 28TH JULY 2006

Intel employees send or read 3m emails a day.
NEW YORK TIMES, 2ND MARCH 2008

People called Paul have appeared on 57 number one singles since the British chart began in 1953; the runner up is John with 54.
BBC NEWS ONLINE, 25TH JULY 2007

From 1987 to 1989, over 100m Garfield suction-cup dolls were sold a year.
NETORAMA

Fewer than 1 per cent of Google searches make use of the 'I'm Feeling Lucky' button.
MAC USER, 4TH OCTOBER 2007

A third to a half of America's Christians have changed denominations in their lives.
PROSPECT, JANUARY 2004

Ian McEwan's novels are more often studied at A-level than those of any other living British author.
BBC ONLINE, 31ST AUGUST 2007

In academic publishing, each additional self-citation by an author increases the number of citations from others by about one after one year, and by about three after five years.
SCIENTOMETRICS

Of the 22 players who made up England's rugby World Cup
final team in 2003, six were privately educated, seven
went to grammar schools and nine to comprehensives.
But two thirds of the British athletes who won medals
at the 2000 Olympics were educated privately.

PROSPECT RESEARCH

Analysis of 49 metropolitan areas in the US shows that the
greater the airtime devoted to country music, the
greater the white suicide rate. The effect is independent
of divorce, southernness, poverty and gun availability.

SCIENCEBLOGS.COM, 5TH DECEMBER 2007

New Zealand and Britain are two of the few countries in
which a majority of married couples practising family
planning opt for male rather than female sterilisation.

EARTH POLICY INSTITUTE

For every insurgent killed in Iraq, 250,000 bullets have been
fired.

WASHINGTON POST, 18TH NOVEMBER 2007

Only 30 countries do not have a religious or ethnic minority
constituting at least 10 per cent of the population.

ECONOMIST.COM, 15TH JULY 2004

Romanians buy more compilation records, proportionally, than
any other nationality. They account for 41 per cent of all
music sales.

IFPI

Six US presidents were born between 1911 and 1924. None was
born between 1925 and 1946, although John McCain,
the 2008 Republican candidate, was born in 1936.

PROSPECT RESEARCH

As of mid-2007, there were 254 branches of Starbucks within 50 miles of central London, compared to 37 within the same distance of central Manchester and 24 for Birmingham.

STARBUCKS

The average Briton spends roughly 6 per cent of his or her waking life watching dramatic performances (television drama, films and plays).

PHILOSOPHY AND LITERATURE, VOLUME 28

In January 2007, the title 'world's oldest person' changed hands three times.

HARPER'S, APRIL 2007

In the US, spending one's old age on cruise ships is almost as cheap as care. The average cost for a person to live on a cruise ship from 80 until death would be $230,497, compared with $228,075 for care.

JOURNAL OF THE AMERICAN GERIATRICS SOCIETY

The average IQ in Germany is 107, the highest in Europe. Serbs
have the lowest IQ, with an average of 89. Britain is in
the middle with 100.

THE TIMES, 27TH MARCH 2006

Sovereignty can prove very lucrative, if you know how to
exploit it. A number of countries, particularly in Central
America and the Caribbean, have done very nicely in recent years by playing Taiwan and China off against each
other. Taiwan is keen to have as many countries as possible recognise it as an independent state, and China, of
course, wants precisely the opposite – and both have
proved happy to back up their diplomacy with hard cash.
Meanwhile, if you were lucky enough to find yourself
one of the non-permanent members of the UN security
council at the time the US and Britain were pressing for
a second resolution that would call for military action
against Iraq, you would have found yourself the object
of intense diplomacy, with large trade and aid packages
being used as leverage to help swing votes. But perhaps
savviest of all has been the south Pacific island of Tuvalu,
population 11,992. Over the past ten years, *Tuvalu has
made millions, first by selling its telephone country code
to American sex hotlines – activity that in 1996 brought
in $1.2m, 10 per cent of the country's national revenue,
according to the* Far Eastern Economic Review *– and
second by exploiting the happy coincidence that its internet domain name – .tv – is of huge value to western
media investors.* According to some estimates, sales of
the domain name doubled the country's national income
for a while. Not everyone was happy, though – a large
proportion of the .tv sales went to pornography companies, something that didn't sit too well in parts of a
country that is 97 per cent Christian.

The Queen became the first head of state to send an email message in 1976.

'SEND: THE HOW, WHY, WHEN AND WHEN NOT OF EMAIL'
BY DAVID SHIPLEY AND WILL SCHWALBE

The richest person in mainland China is Zhang Yin, a paper recycling entrepreneur worth $3.4bn. Zhang, the world's richest self-made woman, is one of 15 billionaires in China.

FINANCIAL TIMES, 10TH OCTOBER 2006

The Valley of Peace cemetery in Najaf, Iraq, is the biggest in the world, covering five square miles and containing over 5m graves.

PROSPECT, NOVEMBER 2004

Women in almost every culture speak in deeper voices than Japanese women. American women's voices are lower than Japanese, Swedish women's lower than American, and Dutch women's lower than Swedish.

'THE HUMAN VOICE' BY ANNE KARPF

The Hungarian physicist Leó Szilárd conceived the idea of a nuclear chain reaction, and thus the creation of the atomic bomb, while waiting at a traffic light on Southampton Row, London – just around the corner from the current location of the *Prospect* offices.

'THE GREAT ESCAPE: NINE JEWS WHO FLED HITLER
AND CHANGED THE WORLD' BY KATI MARTON

New York's department of education has set up a cricket league, with about 600 state secondary school students playing. It is the only state school system in America to offer competitive cricket.

DAILY TELEGRAPH, 7TH APRIL 2008

Over 99.9 per cent of the land on Earth is not occupied by a person at a given time. While 50 to 200 'large' pieces of man-made space debris return to Earth every year, experts know of only one report of a person being hit. Lottie Williams of Tulsa, Oklahoma, was struck on the shoulder in 1997 by a small piece of debris from a discarded piece of a Delta rocket. She was unhurt.

AP, 20TH FEBRUARY 2008

The US delivery company UPS has redesigned its routes to reduce left-hand turns. As a result, the company shaved 30m miles off its deliveries in 2007.

PARADE, 6TH APRIL 2008

A survey in Melbourne found that mild to moderately depressed women enjoy a third more sexual activity than the non-depressed.

HERALD SUN, 20TH MARCH 2008

A 2005 survey in Sweden found that for every two inches more in height, men's suicide rate decreased by 9 per cent. But a more recent study has found an even stronger correlation between male body length at birth and the probability of an attempt at suicide in later life.

WILSON QUARTERLY, SPRING 2008

No private individual currently owns a certified Vermeer painting.

'DISCOVER YOUR INNER ECONOMIST' BY TYLER COWEN

Boeing has a patent on using the gravity of the moon to adjust the orbits of artificial satellites.

SPACE-TRAVEL.COM, 11TH APRIL 2008

Five people were killed by falling icicles in the central Russian town of Samara between 23rd and 25th February 2008.

REUTERS, 26TH FEBRUARY 2008

In a psychological experiment in which subjects were asked to watch a video of a basketball game and to count the number of passes made by one team, half failed to notice that a woman dressed in a gorilla suit was in frame for nine seconds, walking among the players and thumping her chest.

DAILY TELEGRAPH, 5TH MAY 2004